Publish Don't Perish

100 Tips that Improve Your Ability to Get Published

Publish Don't Perish:

100 Tips that Improve Your Ability to Get Published

By
Robert N. Lussier, PhD
Springfield College; Springfield, MA

INFORMATION AGE PUBLISHING, INC.
Charlotte, NC • www.infoagepub.com

Library of Congress Cataloging-in-Publication Data

Lussier, Robert N.
  Publish don't perish : 100 tips that improve your ability to get published
/ by Robert N. Lussier.
      p. cm.
  Includes bibliographical references.
  ISBN 978-1-61735-113-6 (pbk.) – ISBN 978-1-61735-114-3 (hardcover) –
ISBN 978-1-61735-115-0 (e-book)
  1. Scholarly publishing. 2. Communication in learning and
scholarship–Technological innovations. 3. Authorship. 4. Academic
writing. I. Title.
  Z286.S37L87 2010
  070.5–dc22
                                    2010027402

Printed in the United States of America

CONTENTS

PREFACE

Purpose. Today, publish or perish is hitting virtually all colleges and universities. As much as we may love to teach, without publishing we may not get a faculty position, tenure, and promotions. Publishing often affects our salaries and ability to move to a new position. Therefore, the purpose of this book is to help you get your academic work published. Thus, anyone who is interested in ideas that will help them get published, and those who would like to help others publish, will benefit from this book.

    Antecedents. This book is based on more than 25 years of experience as a professor of business management at Springfield College with more than 340 publications including top-tier referred journal articles, editor-selected articles, conference proceedings, best-selling textbooks, textbook supplements, and cases. I've also mentored faculty members from a variety of business schools. But the primary way this book came to be is through my conducting workshops at various conferences and

Publish Don't Perish: 100 Tips that Improve Your Ability to Get Published, pages vii–000
Copyright © 2010 by Information Age Publishing
All rights of reproduction in any form reserved.

colleges and universities. People who benefited from my publishing tips handouts suggested that I turn my great tips into a book to help more doctoral students and faculty members, so I wrote this book for you.

Tips. Although the subtitle of the book is 100 Tips that Improve Your Ability to get Published, you will notice that I have not numbered the tips. There are actually more than 150 tips in this book. The tips are not sequential so it is not really worth the time and effort to try to sequence them to come out with a list of exactly 100 tips. However, if you want to number all the tips, or just the relevant ones to you, go right ahead.

Limitations. I am a professor of business management, so the tips are based on my experience in the field of management. Therefore, some of the tips may not be relevant to your field. However, most of the tips are generic to all academic publishing.

My Personal Guarantee. I can't guarantee you will get published by following my tips, but if you implement my tried and proven methods, you will improve your ability to get published. The book is written at the basic level for doctoral candidates and new faculty. But seasoned authors will get tips that they haven't heard or thought about. If you get just one tip that helps you get published, and I'm confident your will get lots of them, the book was well worth the price. If you don't get any new tips, send me a letter of explanation and a copy of your purchase receipt and I will personally refund your money.

Acknowledgements. One thing I've learned is that when you give you receive. Over the years as I have conducted Publish Don't Perish workshops at conferences and colleges and universities, when I present tips, attendees also share tips with me. Therefore, I'd like to thank the people who have attended my workshops and provided some of the tips included in this book. I got some of the ideas for tips from Emerald, which publishes close to 200 journals. Its website (www.emeraldinsight.com) has a link "For Authors" which gets you to "How-to Guides" with tips.

I'd also like to acknowledge my publisher George Johnson and the staff at Information Age Publishing for the great job in publishing this book.

Contact me. If you have any tips I didn't include, or you would like to give me feedback on the book, I'd like you to contact me.

Dr. Robert N. Lussier
Springfield College
Springfield, MA 01109
(rlussier@spfldcol.edu)

DEDICATION

Although I have had a few good mentors during my education and academic career, I'm dedicating this book to Joel Corman for his great advice and encouragement for more than 25 years. Without the mentorship of Joel Corman, I would not have achieved such a high level of academic success. Thanks again Joel.

Robert N. Lussier

CHAPTER 1

FOUNDATIONS

CHAPTER OVERVIEW

- This book isn't quite like other books you have read, so I start with an explanation of how to use this book.
- Sections two and three lists and briefly explains six different common types of academic publications (with reviews) and types of articles, which will be referred to throughout the book.
- The forth section illustrates how I list publication on my curriculum vitae.
- The next section discuses the first foundation—the importance of a winning attitude to be successful at publishing.
- Section six is the second foundation—persistence; without it you will most likely perish.
- The seventh section is to have multiple projects going at the same time.
- The next section is a brief overview of each of the chapters so you know what is coming.
- The last section provides a summary of the tips presented in the chapter.

CHAPTER OUTLINE

HOW TO USE THIS BOOK

This book is most likely different from other books you have read. You can skip or rush through areas that you are not interested in. More importantly, this book is designed to be applied and used as a reference.

Skip or Rush It

First, although it may be helpful, most of this book does not need to be read in sequence. There may be chapters and sections of the book that are not of interest to you, so skip them. Because this book is written at the level for doctoral students and new faculty, you may already know some of information, so you can skip it or read it over quickly. However, I don't really suggest skipping areas that have some interest for you because there are tips you may not be aware of in sections that seem basic to you. When I've run Publish Don't Perish workshops, I've had tenured full professors tell me that they have gotten some great ideas that will help them in their publishing.

Did you notice the title is not how to read this book? That is because I hope you don't simply read this book; I hope you use it. Like most books, you can simply read it cover-to-cover glancing at or ignoring the boxed items and then self it. There are two ways you can USE this book. You can apply it and use it as a reference book. If you really want to get the most from this book, here is what I recommend.

Applications

The book is designed to engage you, so be interactive. I don't recommend simply reading the material and skipping or rushing through the applications that are "relevant" to you—tips that you don't use, or could improve on, that can help you get published. The applications are questions that get you to think about the publishing tips, if you use them, and how you can improve your ability to get published. The applications are placed in boxes with some space to write in your brief answers. For the tips that relate to you, take the time to answer the applications and write at least a few notes in the space provided.

Reference

After you have read and developed plans to apply the publishing tips, I recommend that you refer to the book as you work on your publications. As I don't have all the tips memorized, I actually do refer to the book contents while publishing. Every so often, it is helpful to go back to the application boxes and to find out if you are implementing your plans. A new read though may also reveal other applications that were not relevant to you earlier.

You may be thinking that this opening section is too basic and obvious. It is. But I have been conducting publishing tips workshops for years and find that the majority of academics don't actually apply the tips and use the material as a reference when they work on publications. So my first tip to you is to actually apply what you learn that relates to you and use the book as a reference. Let's start now with an application.

APPLICATION 1-1 (1)

Do I plan to apply the tips and use the book as a reference source to improve my ability to get published?

_____

_____

_____

_____

TYPES OF ACADEMIC PUBLICATIONS AND REVIEWS

There are at least six different types of publications: refereed journals, editor-selected journals, conference proceedings, books/textbook, textbook supplement, cases with three types of refereed reviews. Here I briefly explain each type of publication. In Chapter 3, we revisit these sources and discuss the pros and cons of each type of publication as an aid to selecting sources of publications—what type of publications can you get? In Chapter 7, I offer specific tips based on the type of publication you are striving for.

Refereed Journal Articles (Peer Reviews)

Article publication decisions are based on reviews by the editor and peers. Another less technical term used is peer-review articles. A refereed journal can use two primary different types of reviews: blind and author known.

The term *blind* review is generally used to indicate that the editor selects reviewers, but the referees do not know the author's name, and vice versa. A number before the word blind indicates how many reviewers assess the work. Thus, a *double blind* review means that at least two reviewers make an assessment of the article, often called a manuscript until it is published as an article.

In the *author known* review, the editor and reviewers know who the authors are, but the authors don't know who the reviewers are. Author known is not blind and is less objective, and it is not commonly used in academic journals, but is used in some trade magazines/journals.

Conference Paper Proceedings (Refereed)

They are commonly called papers that are presented at a conference and published in the proceedings. Proceedings are becoming less often an actual paper form/like a journal and more commonly given on a CD at the conference and also published online at the professional association sponsoring website. Thus, a paper presented that is not in proceedings, is just a presentation, not a publication. Conference papers are commonly refereed. We will discuss professional associations in more detail in the next chapter, and Chapters 3 and 4 have a heavy focus on publishing in refereed journals and proceedings.

Editor-Selected Journal/Magazine Articles and Book Reviews

As the name implies, the decision to publish is only based on an editor review, no peers are involved in the acceptance decision. This type of article is commonly found in non-academic professional association and trade journals and magazines. However, many good journals also include book reviews. So you can get a book review published. Chapter 7 provides tips on writing for practitioners and how to write book reviews.

Authored and Edited Books/Textbooks and Chapters

The primary difference between a book and a textbook is the format, content, and target sales customer. You can also write a chapter in an authored or edited book, and you can edit a book getting others to contribute articles and/or chapters to your edited book. Many book proposals and books are peer reviewed before publishing. Chapter 7 provides tips on publishing authored and edited books.

Textbook Supplements

These are commonly instructor manuals, PowerPoint slides, test bank materials, cases, and exercises that are commonly given away with a book on CD or made available online for professors and/or students; some are sold separately for use with the textbook. Many supplements are not peer reviewed. Chapter 7 provides tips on publishing textbook supplements.

Cases

Cases generally give a fairly detailed real life situation (like a company) that students are asked to analyze. Harvard Business Cases are commonly used in MBA programs. There are at least four primary places to publish cases.

- *Case publishers.* First, you can have a case published through an organization, like Harvard, that will sell it individually.
- *Case journals.* You can publish cases in a special case journal (*Journal of Case Studies* and *Journal of Business Case Studies*).
- *Journals with cases.* Another option is journals that have articles that also publish cases (*Entrepreneurship Theory and Practice*).
- *Textbooks.* A last option is to have your case(s) published in someone else's textbook.

Depending upon the publishing source, the case may or may not be peer reviewed. Chapters 7 and 8 provide tips on publishing cases and textbook supplements.

Prestige of Publications

Generally, I have presented the types of publications in the order of academic prestige, except possibly cases. The rationale is that journal articles and papers contribute new knowledge to your field, and it is generally more difficult to get accepted in a refereed journal than at a conference. Editor-selected articles, books, supplements, and cases generally don't provide any new knowledge to your field, and thus have lower prestige.

Rater
However, there can always be exceptions based on the evaluator who is rating your work. For example, the *Harvard Business Review* is an editor select non-refereed journal. Yet, it is very prestigious to be published in the HBR. If you teach at

Harvard, you may be expected to publish cases. In order to determine the prestige of publications, you need to know the requirements of your school. We will discuss meeting your school's publishing requirements with more details about prestige in Chapter 3.

APPLICATION 1-2 (2)

Which types of publications do I have (or plan to have)? Are there other types of publications I can get? How can I improve?

_____

_____

_____

TYPES OF ARTICLES

There are at least three different types of articles or papers: empirical, conceptual, and informative.

Empirical Articles

They test research question hypotheses base on literature reviews using primary data and commonly report statistical findings. There are also empirical qualitative research articles, such as case studies, that do collect primary in-depth data with a small sample but do not report statistical results. Chapter 8 provides quantitative empirical research information for each stage of the research process.

Conceptual Articles

They are based on secondary data and offer synthesis of the literature and research question propositions with recommendations for empirical study. Some researchers start with a conceptual paper and go on to empirical study.

Informative Articles

They report data, news and/or provide advice for the reader with limited, if any, primary data collection and literature review. Informative articles are also called "how to" articles when they offer advice, which may include some reference to prior empirical and/or conceptual articles. Many academic conferences and journals do not accept informative articles, whereas some do and many trade association journals and magazines prefer informative articles, which are commonly editor selected.

Many professional associations have journals that accept empirical and conceptual articles, such as USASBE's *Entrepreneurship Theory and Practice.* Some have journals exclusively for one type of article. For example, AoM's *Academy of Management Journal* only publishes empirical articles. The *Academy of Management Review* only publishes conceptual articles. The *Academy of Management Perspectives* only publishes informative articles, but they are heavily based on the literature to support advice to executives. There is also the *Academy of Management Learning & Education* that focuses on teaching.

APPLICATION 1-3 (3)

Which types of article do I write (or plan to write)? Are there other types of articles I can get? How can I improve?

_____

_____

_____

Publication Listings on Curriculum Vitae

Here I present ideas from my curriculum vitae (CV). It might give you ideas on developing your own CV. At the top of my curriculum vitae it reads, "In Brief and Table of Contents for CV." The first two pages of my 60 page CV is a summary and the first page includes the following:

Publication Summary (pp. 5–51)

	10	09	08	07	06	05	04	03	Total
Refereed Journal Articles (5–12)		4	3	2	2	4	4	3	59
Editor Selected Articles (13–18)		4	6	0	0	1	1	2	40
Refereed Proceedings (19–38)	2	9	9	7	7	13	11	11	132
Textbooks-one million used (39–43)	2	4	2	2	1	3	2	1	41
Textbook Supplements (44–51)	2	4	1	1	1	1	2	2	70
Totals	6	25	21	12	11	22	20	19	341

If you are thinking that I must not do any, or very little, teaching you are wrong. My teaching load has always been four courses per semester, eight per year. By following my tips, you too can increase your publication productivity.

Here is one selected examples of how I list publications under each of my five categories of publications. Note that I like to use multiple lines for each publication to increase the length of my CV.

Refereed Journal Articles
Robert N. Lussier and Matthew C. Sonfield
   "Founder Influence in Family Business: Analyzing
   Combined Data From Six Diverse Countries"
     JOURNAL OF SMALL BUSINESS STRATEGY
     2009, Spring/Summer, Vol: 20
     Iss:12, pp.103–118.

Editor Selected Articles
Robert N. Lussier and Claudia Halabi

"A Three Level Business Performance Model: An
Empirical Test In Chile"
*SMALL BUSINESS ADVANCEMENT NATIONAL
CENTER NEWSLETTER*
WWW.SBAERletter@sbaer.uca.edu
2009, March 3, Iss: 557-2009, pp. 1-2.

Refereed Proceedings
Matthew C. Sonfield and Robert N. Lussier
"Family Business Generational Stages: A Multi-
National Analysis"
*PROCEEDING OF THE SMALL BUSINESS
INSTITUTE*
*(SBI) Vol. 33, No. 1 Winter Online at
http://www.smallbusinessinstitute.biz*
2009, February 12–14, St. Petersburg, FL,
pp. 143–160.

Textbooks
Robert N. Lussier
*HUMAN RELATIONS IN ORGANIZATIONS:
APPLICATIONS AND SKILL BUILDING 8/e*
2010, Irwin/McGraw-Hill, Burr Ridge, IL

Textbook Supplements
Robert N. Lussier and Christopher Achua
*INSTRUCTOR'S MANUAL to accompany LEADERSHIP:
THEORY, APPLICATIONS, SKILL DEVELOPMENT 4/e*
by Lussier and Achua
2010, South-Western/Thomson, Mason, OH

Your CV
   Depending on your career, you may not want to have publications in each of these categories, and you may have others,
such as cases. I write cases, but they are only in my textbooks,
so they don't count under a separate case category.

If you don't have a lot of publications each year, you may not want to have a summary like I include on my CV.

Publications Heading

If you don't have much variety in the type of publications or not very many publications, you can simply combine all your publications (articles and proceedings) into one category simply listed as publications. But as you progress in your career, if you are successful, it is better to separate articles from proceedings.

Combing Presentations and Publications

If you do present papers or give talks (such as at a Rotary Club meeting) that are not published in proceedings or the professional association's website, and you don't have a strong publication record, a tip is to include presentations and publications together under the combined heading presentations and publications. I do have presentations under that name in another later section "Professional Service" of my CV.

APPLICATION 1-4 (4)

Should I change my CV? How?

_____

_____

_____

_____

A WINNING ATTITUDE

If you really want to be successful at publishing, you need a winning attitude. What is your attitude towards publishing and how can you improve it?

What is Your Attitude Towards Publishing?

Is your attitude more like, "I really don't want to publish" or "I really enjoy (or look forward to) publishing?" Let's face it, if you have a negative attitude towards publishing and you really don't want to publish, your chances of putting in the time and effort to succeed are limited. As research has supported years ago, you can change your attitude, if you want to and work at it.

Being Realistic

When I first starting working on academic empirical research articles, I wanted to help entrepreneurs know the factors that distinguish success from failure. I wanted to contribute to having more successful entrepreneurs. Great ideals and lots of publications followed. However, let's be realistic and honest. Most entrepreneurs don't read academic journals, our real audience is usually other professors. For one thing, most practitioners don't understand the statistics and the articles usually don't offer any clear advice. The business failure rate has not gone down because of my research, so I haven't saved the small business world. Is or will your research save your field of study? If you are like the vast majority of us academics, the answer is no. So let's not take ourselves too seriously.

My Attitude

I'm going to tell you my attitude towards publishing. Some people don't agree with my attitude, and that's fine, but it does work, at least for me. Without a positive winning attitude, I would not have more than 340 publications.

My basic attitude is that publishing is a game; it's fun. I enjoy getting published (winning) and seeing my name it print. I pride myself in that fact I have contributed to my field of small business research and that my textbooks have been used to teaching management to more than one million students (not to mention the royalties). People from all over the US and 57 other countries have contacted me about my publications.

Improving Your Attitude Towards Publishing

Here are four ideas to keep in mind that may help you to maintain a winning attitude.

1. **Publishing benefits**. What are the benefits of our academic publishing? I've mentioned some of my benefits. In general, we do contribute to our field of academic study. We get satisfaction, recognition, jobs, tenure, promotions, raises, travel and other benefits.

2. **It's a numbers game**. One statement that I have always liked is, "deans can't read, but they can count." To a large extent, publishing is a numbers game. There's that word game again. I like it because games are supposed to be enjoyable and winning (publishing) is fun. So my tip is to keep focusing on the positive side of publishing—it's fun and rewarding! As a tenured full professor, I don't publish because I have to, I publish because I want to, as it is enjoyable; it helps meet my need for achievement.

3. **A view of publishing.** Another way that I view publishing is like pregnancy. I know, I'm a man and can't fully understand it, but here is my analogy. Working on a publication can take a long time, sometimes years. The actually work on the publication is not always enjoyable, at times it hurts, but I keep my eyes set on the end result. When I see the publication, I'm really proud. That's my baby—I did that! All the hard work is well worth the time and effort. The big difference is that unlike having babies you usually can't stop at one or two. But like a boxer, you do learn to roll with the punches and accept and continue the hard work on your way to the next winning publication.

4. **Focus on the positive.** If you need an attitude adjustment, when you think about publishing, think of it as being enjoyable; its fun think of the great benefits—like getting, keeping, or advancing in your job. Think of my analogy of it's a game or like a pregnancy, or develop your own that helps keep your attitude positive towards publishing. Whenever you start to think negatively about publishing, replace those thoughts with your positive statements. Learning the tips throughout the

book can also help you develop a more positive attitude towards publishing.

APPLICATION 1-5 (5)

What is my attitude toward publishing? How can I improve it?

_____

_____

_____

PERSISTENCE PAYS

If you haven't learned it yet, you will have to deal with rejection of your work for publication, so thick skin helps. You will also need to revise and resend your work to be successful.

Deal With Rejection; It Takes Thick Skin

If you view publishing as a game, you should know the saying that you can't win them all. You can't expect that everything you send out will be accepted for publication by the first place you send it. We must accept and deal with the fact that our work will be rejected for publication by some sources. Even the best get rejected. I have more than 340 publications that I count and record on my curriculum vitae. However, I don't keep track of my rejects, but I'd guess it's probably in the range of 1,500. My rejection rate was very high to start, but as I learned the game the hard way through my mistakes, my rejection rate decreased dramatically. I wrote this book for you so that you can avoid some of my mistakes and to give you tips I learned from others over 30 years.

Ways to View Success and Failure

If you talk to successful people in any field, they will tell you they have had failures along the way. Winston Churchill's definition of success applies so well to publishing; *Success* is the ability to go from failure to failure without losing your enthusiasm. Don't take rejection personally. It's not you that is getting rejected—it's just the one thing that you want to get published at this one source. One source may not want to, but another may think it is great.

Publishing is actually great because your work that is rejected by one source can be sent to other sources until it is accepted. So ultimately, you don't really fail in the end. View rejections as a false start not *failure*, it's an opportunity to improve your work and learn from mistakes.

Keep Reworking and Resending

Getting back to the game, you should know the saying that quitters never win and winners never quit, and if at first you don't succeed, keeping on trying until you do succeed. As Jack Welch said, it's about getting back up on the horse, and learning from your mistakes. I've seen so many people get rejected and just give up. All their hard work is in vain. It took me more than two years to get my first good journal article from my dissertation published and to get an editor to agree to publish my *Management Fundamentals* textbook.

How to deal with rejection

Thick skin helps us to avoid getting hurt, and time heals wounds. Common approaches to rejection is to read the letter, feel the pain of rejection, and use your defense mechanisms such as telling yourself that the editor and/or reviewers don't know what they are talking about or that they are wrong. Let the letter sit for a few days to a week (careful here, with many people, the longer they wait the harder it is to revise and resend). Next, re-read the letter being objective and seeking feedback on how you can improve the work. Now revise based on the feedback and resend to another source.

Down the line

It is common to start by sending your work to a high level source. If rejected, you keep sending it to other same level sources, and then to lower level sources until you get it published. I've had papers rejected from top level conferences, but found lower level conferences at which to present them. I sent one article to around 20 journals, over a two year period, before getting it accepted.

If you can apply the tips throughout the book, stay persistent, and learn from your mistakes you should get published, and the number of rejections you get will decrease over time.

APPLICATION 1-6 (6)

Am I persistent? How do I deal with rejection? How can I improve?

_____

_____

_____

HAVING WORK IN EACH STAGE OF THE PUBLISHING PROCESS

How full is your pipeline? Your pipeline has five stages of publications.

1. Ideas and proposals;
2. In the process of conducting/writing;
3. Out to review or revise and re-submit;
4. Accepted, waiting to be published—in press;
5. Published.

Some people seem to think that they can simply work on one project at a time taking it through the five stages. At this rate, you may not be highly successful at publishing proceedings and journal articles. I do plan my next book as well. Thus, my tip is to have at least one, and preferably more, projects at each of the first four stages.

Have a *written list* with the first four stages (publications go on your curricular vitae). My file is called Research in Process, but I like Pipeline too. Once you have work in the various stages, you will understand the need to keep track of your work. Be sure to keep track of the dates that you send out your work for review so that you know when to follow-up if you don't get a decision on time.

The major benefit of a full pipeline is that you have a constant flow of publications. A second benefit is the motivational factor. Getting back to rejection, it's not unusual for me to get a rejection letter, but a short time later I get an acceptance or actual publication. The consistent wins help offset the rejections and keep me going strong.

APPLICATION 1-7 (7)

Do I (have or plan to) develop a pipeline with work in each stage? How can I improve my pipeline?

_____

_____

_____

_____

THE REST OF THE BOOK

Now that we have a basic foundation, we can move onto more details related to these foundations.

Chapter 2 provides basic aids to publishing including getting a mentor, writing proposals, having your work reviewed, proofreading, and publishing through professional associations.

Chapters 3 and 4 focus primarily on publishing proceedings and journal articles. The tips can help you to select topics and publication sources, and to match the publication sources you send your work to, so that you can increase your chances of getting accepted.

Chapter 5 provides time management tips that can increase your publishing productivity including scheduling classes and time to work on publishing.

Chapter 6 has tips that will help you to multiple your publications and revise your work including coauthors, publication, progression, and making multiple use of your sample.

Chapter 7 provides tips for refereed sources of publication, including proceedings and presentations (how to get feedback to improve your work), journals (how to handle the revise and resubmit), and case studies (writing and publishing them).

Chapter 8 focuses on tips for publishing in non-refereed sources, including editor selected journals, edited books, book reviews, textbooks, and textbook supplements.

Chapter 9 presents the parts of empirical research papers/articles to be sure you include all the relevant information to improve your chances of acceptance. It is a good reference source to use during the entire research process. I use it myself.

SUMMARY OF TIPS

- To get the most from this book, you need to actually apply the tips and use this book as a reference when you work on your publications.
- Select the appropriate type of publications and reviews that match your career goals.
- Consider the prestige of the source of publication.
- Show your publications on your CV to look your best—use headings for each type of publication or presentations.
- Use multiple lines for each publication listed to increase the length of your CV.
- Develop a winning attitude towards publishing.
- Remember that success is the ability to go from failure to failure without losing your enthusiasm for publishing.
- Persistence is needed for successful publishing; keep reworking and resending.

- Deal with rejection; get back to writing and develop thick skin.
- Have work in each stage of the publishing process

CHAPTER 2

PUBLISHING ASSISTANCE

CHAPTER OVERVIEW

In this chapter, I present some sources of assistance beginning with mentors.

- The second section focuses on the role of professional associations as a means of publications and other benefits.
- The third section discusses the use of proposals, reviewers, and having your completed work pre-reviewed before sending it for publication.
- The last two sections get into basic guidelines about writing and proofreading your work to provide assistance in getting your work published.

CHAPTER OUTLINE

I.   Mentors
     Get a Mentor
     Publish as a Doctoral Student

II. Professional Associations
     Membership Benefits and Conferences
     Read Journals You Want to Publish in
     Professional Association Activity and Publishing

III. Using Proposals and Reviewing
     Write a Proposal for All Research
     Have Your Proposal Reviewed
     Pre-Reviewing and Revising

IV. Writing Guidelines
     Grammar
     Paragraphs and Sentences
     Punctuation—Commas

V.   Proofreading Guidelines
     Proofreading Tips
     Getting Proofreaders

MENTORS

Two tips here are to get a mentor or be a mentor, and if you are a doctoral student, start publishing now.

Get a Mentor

My next tip is to get at least one good mentor, or be a mentor if you are advanced in your career. Ask your professors and more senior faculty colleagues to be your mentor. Before you ask someone to be your mentor, it is a good idea to decide what role you want your mentor to play for you. Mentors can have a few different roles.

Advice
You can have a mentor with the role of just giving you career advice. Any time you want experienced advice during your career, contact your mentor and discuss what is going on and get his or her advice.

Reviewer
As will be discussed in this chapter, you should have proposals reviewed and your work pre-reviewed before you send it out for publication. Thus, you can ask your mentor to be a reviewer of your work. Mentorees should also give back to mentors, so you can also ask to be a reviewer for your mentor.

Coauthor
Your mentors can also be coauthors with you. If you want to coauthor with them, find mentors with similar research interest to you. Don't expect mentors to just hand you publications. In a mentor-coauthor situation, you are not on an equal basis. You are seeking the help of your mentor, and in return you are offering coauthorship for the help getting published. You need to approach mentors with the willingness to do most of the work. I've approached mentors in two different ways.

1. *Your ideas.* The first way is to approach your mentor is with your idea for a publication. The role of mentor is to help you improve your work by giving detailed input at each stage of the process as coauthor. In this case, you should suggest being first author.
2. *Their ideas.* The second approach is to ask them if they have an idea for a publication that they have been too busy to get to, they often have ideas. Your role is to do the work with the input of the mentor who is the coauthor. In this case, if it's truly the mentor's ideas, you can discuss ranking of authorship.

Yes, it's like the dissertation advisor process but for this work they get to be a coauthor of the publication of the paper or article. When mentors get the incentive to be a coauthor they usually do a much better job than a quick review, and you get it back in less time.

As your need for mentoring help decreases and you become coauthors of equal status, you share equally in the work. You can also progress to the point of not needing the help of your mentor and publishing without help. It looks good on your CV to have some solo authored publications. In Chapter 6, coauthorship is discussed with tips for successful team work.

Publish as a Doctoral Student

As a new doctoral student, my attitude was I will wait until I graduate before I start to publish empirical research. Luckily, I had a few good mentors Joel Corman (Suffolk University MBA professor) and David Morris (University of New Haven dissertation advisor) that gave me this tip. Don't wait until you have a faculty position to get active in a professional association. Attend professional association conferences and present papers that are published in proceedings.

Publishing before graduating is now the norm in many fields. If it's not the norm in your field, it will give you an advantage in landing a faculty position. I attended many conferences with my mentor Joel Corman and coauthored several papers and journal articles before and after getting my doctorate.

APPLICATION 2-1 (8)

Do I have a mentor? What role do I want my mentor to play? How can I improve in this area?

_____

_____

_____

_____

PROFESSIONAL ASSOCIATIONS

If you aren't already a member of at least one professional association and attending conferences, my tip is to join at least one because they are a source of both conference proceedings and referred journal publications. Doctoral students usually get discount membership rates. Faculty members can tell you about appropriate associations for your career path, or do an online search.

Membership Benefits and Conferences

In addition to publishing in proceedings, membership and conference there are many benefits. Benefits can vary widely based on the needs and wants of the members. So here are some of the many benefits. Conferences may be a great place to:

- Learn what the latest hot topics are in your field.
- Find out what goes on at other colleges and universities.
- Network to find mentors, coauthors, and faculty positions.
- Get career services. Some colleges and universities conduct interviews during their conferences.
- Attend special sessions for doctoral students and new faulty.

- Get financial support for your dissertation or other research.
- Win awards for a variety of reasons.
- Get journals.

Read Journals You Want to Publish in

Let's provide a little more detail on journals. In addition to holding conferences and publishing papers in their proceedings, professional associations tend to have journals. But there are also journals that are not sponsored by professional associations. My tip here is to read the journals you want to publish in because it helps you to publish in them. Chapter 4, matching publications sources, will provide more tips in this area.

It is common to receive journals as part of the membership fee of the professional association. When you attend the conference, the membership fee may be included in the total conference fee, so you get the journals at no additional cost. However, if you don't attend the conference, it is often less costly to join or renew your membership than it is to subscribe to the journals. I like having hard copies of the journals, but you can go through your library or maybe directly online to the journal's web site to read the journals you want to publish in.

Professional Association Activity and Publishing

Here I will illustrate my professional association activity and publication relationship through sharing my own experience. I'm an ongoing active member of the Small Business Institute® (SBI). I attend the regional and national conferences and present papers that are published in its proceedings. I served on the board for several years, was a regional officer, and have been the program chair at regional conferences. The SBI has two journals (*Journal of Small Business Strategy* and *SBI Journal*), which I read and have published in, and I am currently a reviewer for *JSBS*. For this work and my publication success, I was awarded the SBI's highest award—fellow. Thus, my SBI membership continues to be a source of many conference and journal publications. I would like to acknowledge that it was my mentor Joel Corman that brought me to my first SBI conference, and it was great to be introduced to several people by a person well known and respected by the membership.

I am also a member of the United States Association of Small Business and Entrepreneurship (USASBE). For a few years, I attended its national conference to present papers that were published in its proceedings. I maintain my membership to receive its two journals (*Small Business Management* and *Entrepreneurship Theory and Practice*), which I continue to read and publish in. I am also a member of the Academy of Management (AoM) so that I can read, and reference, its four journals. I occasionally present at three other conferences when they are held locally.

APPLICATION 2-2 (9)

Have I joined one or more professional associations? Do I read journals I want to publish in? How can I improve in this area?

_____

_____

_____

USING PROPOSALS AND REVIEWING

Tips here include writing a proposal for all your research and have it reviewed, and to have your work pre-reviewed and revise it according before you send it in for publication review.

Write a Proposal for All Research

As a doctoral candidate, the dissertation is a critical criterion for graduation. It is common to have a dissertation committee of three members who have to first approve the topic and then the research proposal. The research proposal helps to ensure that your research topic is a good one and that your methodology for completing the research is appropriate.

However, after graduation most people seem to think that they don't need to write any more research proposals. Faculty members may discuss their ideas with others (often limited to coauthors), but they tend to skip the written proposal and go right into conducting research. People often find out that their topic and/or methods are really not good enough to get published, or at least at the level sought. If you want to increase your chances of getting published, my tip is to treat ALL empirical research like a dissertation.

Write at least a simple outline type of proposal for every research study you plan to conduct. Yes. *Write* down your ideas to make sure you have a clear idea of your research question/purpose and what your methodology will be.

Answer the So What Question

The proposal should answer these four questions:

1. Why is this topic important?
2. Why is this research needed? What is the gap in the literature that you are filling by making a new contribution to your topic?
3. What is the purpose/hypothesis of your study?
4. What are the implications of your research? Who can benefit and how because of your study?

Your answers should be backed up by references based on a good literature review.

Methods

The methods should include:

- Participants and procedures for data collection.
- Measurement—a list of all variables with operational definitions.

- Statistical analyses—which tests will you run to test your hypotheses?

We will discuss answering the so what question and methods in more detail in the last chapter, 9, empirical research. Chapter 9 actually includes tips for each stage of the research process.

Have Your Proposal Reviewed

Have your proposal peer reviewed by at least three good qualified people. Coauthors don't count as reviewers, and if you have them, have coauthors get three reviews, too. Try to get written feedback for improvements, but at least discuss your ideas with others and make their suggested improvement (revising) before you begin data collection.

Who to ask to review your proposal? People to ask include your mentors, dissertation committee and faculty members, faculty colleagues where you teach, and other colleges and universities, including your doctoral friends. Try to form alliances through which you review each other's work.

Some colleges and universities have a faculty member who is considered the expert in research. The expert often gets release time from teaching to help faculty publish. If you have this person available, get a review. If your college or university does not have an expert, try to get one. Are you strong in research methods and statistics? If so, consider applying to be the expert for release time.

Pre-Reviewing and Revising

Another common mistake that academics make is to conduct the study and then to send it to the source of publication without having it pre-reviewed. The result is often a rejection. Thus, my tip is to make sure you have your completed study pre-reviewed. You can go back to your research proposal reviews, but it is often helpful to get at least one reviewer that is not already familiar with your study. I also suggest getting copies of the journal's actual reviewer forms to give to your pre-reviewers. Getting copies of reviewer forms is discussed in Chapter 4.

After having your work pre-reviewed and before sending it out for publication, you obviously make the suggested improvements (revising), but you also need to proofread your work to make corrections.

APPLICATION 2-3 (10)

Do I (or plan to) develop proposals and have them reviewed before starting my research? Do I have my completed works pre-reviewed before submitting them for publication? How can I improve in these areas?

_____

_____

_____

_____

WRITING GUIDELINES

Let's get down to basics and review grammar, rhetoric, and punctuation. This section can be especially relevant to you if English is your second language, or you don't remember the basics. If you are not sure when to use a comma, be sure to read the section on punctuation.

Grammar

Grammar refers to the rules for using the following eight parts of speech:

1. *Nouns* are the names of people, places, or things.
2. *Pronouns* take the place of nouns.
3. *Verbs* are the action words in sentences. There are also linking and auxiliary verbs (e.g., *be, have,* and *do*). Verbs

      have number (singular or plural), which must agree with that of the accompanying noun or pronoun, tense (past, present, future), and voice (active or passive).

4. *Adjectives* modify, or give more information about, nouns.

5. *Adverbs* tell something about a verb, an adjective, or another adverb.

6. *Prepositions* (e.g., *to, of, for, at, by, as, on, in, before, after*) relate nouns or pronouns to other parts of a sentence.

7. *Conjunctions* (e.g., *and, but, or, nor, so, yet, because*) connect two words or parts of a sentence together.

8. An *interjection* is a word used to express feelings (e.g., wow for surprise or ouch for pain). Interjections are not commonly used in business and technical writing.

The various parts of speech are used to construct sentences, which have the following parts: The subject is a noun or a pronoun and is the person or thing that performs an action or is described in the sentence. The predicate consists of the main verb and any accompanying verbs, which express an action or describe the subject, along with complement(s) and modifier(s). Most sentences include at least one complement: a direct object, an indirect object, a subject complement, or an object complement. Modifiers include both adjectives (which modify nouns or pronouns) and adverbs (which modify verbs, adjectives, or other adverbs). Connectives join elements of sentences together; prepositions and conjunctions are connectives.

Paragraphs and Sentences

    Syntax is related to grammar as it is the arrangement of words, phrases, and clauses to form sentence structure. A sentence needs a subject (a noun or a pronoun) and a verb, and it often also includes modifiers (adjectives and adverbs) and connectives (prepositions and conjunctions) to convey meaning. A phrase is a group of words that does not form a complete sentence. A clause is a group of words that includes a subject and a verb and often could stand alone as a sentence. Rhetoric is also related to grammar because it refers to the principles and rules of effective writing. The two keys to syntax and rhetoric are the paragraph and sentence.

Paragraphs

Paragraphs should have only one main idea. Start with a topic sentence to introduce the idea, and follow with sentences that develop the main idea. A well-written paragraph organizes the main idea with points flowing from one another in a logical sequence building on the one main idea. You can do this by defining terms, adding information, providing explanation, giving examples, presenting data, comparing, and contrasting studies.

Sentences

Sentences should include only one idea, and that idea should relate to the paragraph's topic sentence. Write to be understood so that every sentence makes sense; it should be easy to read and understand. If your sentence is too short, add to it or combine sentences. If it's too long, split it. An important part of sentences is punctuation, which is our next topic after length. Proofreading is also important, and you get proofread tips after punctuation.

Length

Paragraphs and sentence length should vary, and be similar to the general length of the paragraphs and sentences in the targeted source of publication. But any time you change ideas, you need a new paragraph to develop the new main idea. However, for general business writing, I have developed the 1–5–15 writing rule that states that paragraphs should express 1 idea with an average of 5 sentences with 15 words each.

Punctuation—Commas

Punctuation is the use of special marks—commas, semicolons, colons, dashes, parentheses (commonly used to cite authors and dates of references in articles), and brackets—to group words, phrases, and clauses. I'll focus on the comma, which is the most important mark of internal punctuation, and commas are used incorrectly more frequently than any of the others.

To simplify the use of your understanding of commas, here are three major uses of commas:

1. Commas separate items in a series. A series contains three or more parallel words, phrases, or clauses. Do not use a comma with a series of two.

   WRONG: Smith studied the age of participants, and the length of their illnesses. (Series of two)

   CORRECT: Smith studied the age of participants and the length of their illnesses.

   CORRECT: Smith studied the age of participants, the length of their illnesses, and their incomes. (Series of three)

2. Commas precede coordinating conjunctions that join clauses. Conjunctions join related ideas, and using a coordinating conjunction to join related clauses can help you to avoid a series of short, choppy sentences. The primary coordinating conjunctions are and, but, or, nor, yet, for, and so.

   WRONG: Smith studied age and he also studied length of illness. (Could be two sentences)

   CORRECT: Smith studied age, and he also studied length of illness.

   Testing. To test if you have correctly used a comma with a coordinating conjunction, replace the comma and conjunction with a period. If the result is two complete sentences, the comma is used correctly. If you do not have two complete sentences, omit the comma, because the conjunction is most likely connecting words or phrases rather than clauses. In other words, every time to use the word and (or, nor, yet, for, so) look to the left and right of it. If you have a sentence on both sides, use the comma. If you don't have sentences on both sides, don't use the comma because you have a series of two.

3. Commas set off supplemental (less important) words or phrases at the beginning, middle, or end of sentences—or create a pause. A pause can give the reader a chance to take a breath. Like when speaking, we take a pause. So the comma tells the reader when to pause. A preposition (to, if, when, before, etc.) and the words that follow it form a prepositional phrase.

    Beginning of the sentence. When a sentence begins with a prepositional phrase, the phrase is set off by having a comma following it. The phrase can often be moved to the middle or end of the sentence, where it does not need to be set off by a comma, as shown below.

    WRONG: On the test of team skills the average score was 70%.

    CORRECT: On the test of team skills, the average score was 70%.

    CORRECT: The average scored was 70% on the test of team skills.

    Middle of the sentence. A comma is also used to set off a word or phrase that provides supplemental information about some part of a sentence. Supplemental information is information that is not necessary to the basic meaning of the sentence; if it were deleted from the sentence, the sentence would still be grammatically correct.

    WRONG: To improve conflict resolution skill the weakest area participants should confront others more often.

    CORRECT: To improve conflict resolution skill, the weakest area, participants should confront others more often.

    NOTE: To improve conflict resolution skill, participants should confront others more often. (A grammatically correct sentence)

End of the sentence. Words or phrases that provide supplemental information can also be located at the end of a sentence.

WRONG: Smith controlled for age which makes the study more robust.

CORRECT: Smith controlled for age, which makes the study more robust.

Testing. In summary, words or phrases that provide supplemental information can be located at the beginning, middle, or end of a sentence. Use the test of removing the word or phrase to see whether the sentence retains its grammatical form and basic meaning in order to determine whether to insert a comma or commas.

APPLICATION 2-4 (11)

How can I improve my writing?

_____

_____

_____

_____

PROOFREADING GUIDELINES

One thing to remember is that the publishing editors and reviewers tend to look for reasons to reject your work, rather than to look for reasons to accept it. If you send in work with typos, English, and other errors you are giving the reviewers reasons to reject your work.

Review vs. Proofreading

Pre-reviewers often don't take the time to correct these errors (proofread). The reviewer's job is to focus on content accuracy. It is your job to focus on sentence accuracy. Thus, my tip is to make sure you proofread your work and to have your work proofread by others before submitting it for publication.

Proofreading Tips

Spelling and Grammar Check

Use your word processing spell and grammar check, but that should only be the beginning. A common mistake is to spend hours pushing to finish the paper, followed by a quick spell check and read through. The work is sent for review—with errors.

Don't Proofread Your Work When You Are Tired

Take a day to get a fresh perspective before editing and revising (content improvements) and proofreading (sentence errors) your work.

Sentence Focus

When you proofread, focus on each individual sentence looking for errors in:

- Typos and English—punctuation and easy to read
- Length—too long (split it) or too short (and to or combine sentences)
- Statistics or other math
- References

Separate Proofreading Focus

You may want to look for these different types of errors separately. For example, I proof for typos and English including sentence length together. I check to make sure my results section stats are the same as the Tables separately.

Checking References

I also make sure that each reference cited in the paper is also listed in the reference section, and make sure the author names and years both match correctly in both places. Professor Lloyd Fernald, University of Central Florida, reviews journal articles. Lloyd told me the first thing he does is look for reference accuracy. If he finds citations in the paper that are missing from the reference section, or references listed that are not cited in the paper, he essentially determines that the work is sloppy and that he will most likely end up rejecting it.

To check references, all you need to do is have the paper and the list of references. As you go through the paper finding citations, go to the list of references to make sure it matches and correct any errors, and be sure to check it off on the list of references. When you get to the end of the paper, every citation in the paper will be in the list of references. If you have any extra references not listed in the paper, you can delete the reference or put it in the paper. This method is also used to check for the use of *et al.* in APA and other styles.

Proofread on the Computer then Again On Hard Copy

I proofread first on the computer making the corrections. Then, I print out the paper and proof it again, ending by going back to the computer to make the changes.

Have Others Proofread It (Hard Copy?)

Next, I print out the work and give it to our department administrative assistant to proofread. Note that I don't give her my e-file because I want to make sure that what she corrects is accurate. I only make the changes in my e-file that I agree with. I once gave a generic cover letter to a person who incorrectly changed "personnel" manger to "personal" manager and printed 300 copies. Although you can use tracking changes to see what was done, I think it takes longer to check the e-file, take out any changes I don't agree with, and to remove the tracking record. Also, I once reviewed a paper that had the tracking changes still visible in the file—which gave me a reason to reject the paper.

Getting Proofreaders

Three usually no cost options are:

1. *Administrative assistance*—secretaries.
2. *College writing centers* that helps students—may help faculty too.
3. *Friends and family.*

Although they may not tend to be helpful with content, they are often good at finding typos and English errors that you and pre-reviewers miss. If you are really weak at writing, you may hire a professional to proofread your work, such as paying an English professor.

As stated in Chapter 1, this book is meant to be a reference source. Therefore, you may want to refer back to this chapter when you are writing and proofreading your work.

APPLICATION 2-5 (12)

Do I (or plan to) proofread before submitting by work for publication? Do I have others proofread my work, and who will I get to proofread for me? How can I improve in this area?

_____

_____

_____

SUMMARY OF TIPS

- Get a mentor for advice.
- Have a mentor review your work.
- Have a mentor as a coauthor.
- Publish as a doctoral student.
- Join professional associations.
- Read journals you want to publish in.
- Write a proposal for all your research that answers the so-what question.
- Have your proposals reviewed.
- Have your work pre-reviewed before submitting for publication.
- Write clearly using proper English.
- Proofread your work and have others proofread your work to make sure there are no errors before submitting for publication.

CHAPTER 3

SELECTING TOPICS AND PUBLICATION SOURCES

CHAPTER OVERVIEW

- The first section presents the theme that runs throughout the chapter; you need to know your schools publishing requirements.
- The second section addresses meeting your school requirements through your niche.
- The next section gives tips on selecting topics that are publishable.
- The fourth section presents the different sources of publications and the pros and cons of each.
- The fifth section explains methods for finding the right journal for your article. Submitting to the right journals increases your acceptance rate.
- The last section discusses the question or quality vs. quantity of publications, with my advice. It ends with providing ways of judging the quality of journals.

Publish Don't Perish: 100 Tips that Improve Your Ability to Get Published, pages 40–63
Copyright © 2010 by Information Age Publishing

CHAPTER OUTLINE

   I. Knowing School Requirements
       Can You Meet the Requirement?—Don't Perish
       Don't Fool Yourself
       Leaving is not Career Failure
  II. Finding Your Niche
 III. Selecting Topics
       Ask Others, Editors and Special Issues
       Conferences
       Literature Search
       Further Research
 IV. Selecting Publication Sources
       Refereed Journal Articles
       Conference Paper Proceedings
       Editor Selected Articles and Book Reviews
       Authored and Edited Books/Textbooks and Chapters
       Textbook Supplements
       Cases
   V. Finding the Appropriate Journal
       Follow the Reference Chain
       Ask Others, Conferences and Journals
       Publication Listings
       Read the Author Guidelines
 VI. Quality vs. Quantity
       Start with Quantity and Quality then Go for Quality
       Determining Quality

KNOWING SCHOOL REQUIREMENTS

The selection of topics and sources is based on knowing the requirements of your school. Your school refers to which colleges and universities you want to apply to or for which you are currently a professor. Getting back to publishing as a game, would you get into a game not knowing how to win and what the rules are? *You MUST know the publication requirements.*

Some schools have written requirements that specify the number of publications (quantity) that are expected per year and the specific conference proceedings and journals (quality) you need to publish in to attain tenure and promotion. If the school doesn't have written requirements, ask the dean, department chair, senior faculty, and people on the tenure and promotion committee what the requirements are. Schools vary greatly in their publication requirements, but generally the higher the prestige of the school the greater the publication requirements. The general trend is giving less importance to proceedings and greater importance on refereed journals, and to top-tier journals. The focus of this chapter is more related to publishing in refereed conference proceedings and journals.

Can You Meet the Requirement?—Don't Perish

Meeting the requirements is obvious, but it is often easier said than done. Before you take a faculty position, find out the publication requirements and do a "realistic" self-assessment to determine if you can meet the requirements. For example, if you are expected to publish in top tier journals (such as the *Academy of Management*), can you publish in this level journal? Even if you say yes as I did once, once isn't enough. Most schools only consider publications within the last five years, so the one-time home run is forgotten, or it's the old what-have-you-done-lately that matters.

If You Can't, Leave Before You Perish Without Tenure
If you are doing a job search, try to find a school at which you can meet the publication requirements. If you know you can't meet the publication requirements, and there are no other jobs take it. But go into it not expecting to stay and keep searching for a job that is a good match.

If you thought you could meet the requirements, but you can't, realize it, and do a job search. Although you should not need them to know if you are meeting the publishing requirements, most schools have pre-tenure reviews. If you are not meeting the requirements, you are better off leaving before you are denied tenure.

Don't Fool Yourself

I've met and heard about several early stage faculty members who just don't get it. My tip is don't fool yourself, but I'm not sure how to tell you to be realistic. Maybe four examples will help.

I Can Do It
Even though they get pre-tenure reviews stating that they are not meeting the publication requirements, they unrealistically tell themselves, "I will meet the requirement next year." Only to end up being denied tenure.

They Will Count Proceedings
I know a colleague through a conference who told me of his concern that his school had increased the publishing standard after he was hired. The new requirement was to publish one refereed journal article every two years. He had never published any journal articles. I suggested to him that he stop going to conferences just about every month and focus on a journal article. He was fooling himself into thinking that the school would accept 10 or 20 proceedings as, or equal to, one refereed journal article. When he went up for tenure, he couldn't believe he was denied.

Others could clearly see it coming, so why was he fooling himself? Like 10 master's degrees don't equal one doctorate degree, 100 proceedings don't equal one refereed journal article. Five refereed journal articles in low-level journals don't equal one in a specified top-tier journal.

My Teaching Will Save Me

I've meet people who are great teachers that get off-the-chart student evaluations. Student love them; they win teaching awards. They seem to think that great teaching will take the place of publishing. Unless you have it in writing from the provost and dean, don't believe it.

I know a woman who is a great teacher, but has a weak publishing record. She was denied tenure at two different schools. She took a job as a new MBA director thinking that her publishing could slide as she developed the program. Now in her fourth job she told me that she finally gets it; she found a mentor that can help her publish refereed journal articles.

My College Service Will Save Me

There are people who like to serve on college committees. College service is often a requirement for tenure and promotion, but it will not take the place of publishing. Some people combine the good teaching and college service to replace meeting publishing requirement in vain. Let's face it, service on committees takes time away from publishing. Which is more important at your school? Put your time and effort where it counts—in most cases publishing. My tip here is that if you are going to serve on a committee, find one that doesn't do much work and doesn't meet often. Like with many publication listings, they may count equal to committees that do a lot of work.

Leaving Is Not Career Failure

If you haven't been denied tenure, you haven't failed. You gained some experience, but you are not at the right school for your career. Do a job search and find a school at which you can meet the publication requirements, and you will be happier and have a successful career.

I met a colleague at a conference who told me he taught at Yale University. A couple of years later, I asked him how things were going at Yale, and he told me is now at a different university. Although he had a number of publications, he didn't meet the requirements of Yale so his pre-tenure review was not good, so he looked for a job with lower publication requirements. He received a good recommendation from Yale because they knew he would succeed at the other university. The other university was glad to have him, as he is one of the top publishers for the school. Needless to say, when he was going through the experience is was very difficult. But after the move, he realized that things worked out for the best. Although he is not at as prestigious a school, he is near the top of the publishing ranking, rather than the bottom where he was. His worries about performance reviews and getting tenured and advancing through to full professor were gone. He is happy.

APPLICATION 3-1 (13)

What are the publishing requirements at my school, or the type of school I want to publish for? Can I realistically meet the requirements? Should I leave? How can I improve?

_____

_____

_____

_____

FINDING YOUR NICHE

Going hand-in-hand with knowing school requirements is finding a niche for your work. So your niche is the source that will publish your work. Your niche has at least three parts, or questions to answer.

- The first part of finding your niche is to answer the question, "What is your level?" Can you get published in top-tier conference proceedings and refereed journals? If not, why waste your time? Shooting for your level generally results is more publications and less rejection.
- The next part of finding your niche is identifying what type of papers/articles/books can you write? Can you write empirical, conceptual, and/or informative articles?
- Last, is there as niche within your field of interest? For example, the Academy of Management (AoM) and American Psychological Association (APA) have many divisions, sub-fields, or topic areas.

Can you understand how your niche relates to selecting a topic and source of publication? We will discuss selecting in this chapter in the next couple of sections. But first, I'll share my level with you to help illustrate the process. I'm not at the highest level of publications, but I exceed my school's publishing requirements through my niche.

My Niche

I began my early doctoral student time by writing a few informative how-to articles in editor-selected magazines, which included no literature review. However, I found out that this type of publication was given little, if any, weight in most of the schools I was interested in working for. At this time, I couldn't write empirical or conceptual articles because I hadn't had any research methods and statistics classes yet. During my student days, I did get a few low-level conference proceedings and a refereed journal article published.

Based on my dissertation, *Small Business Success vs. Failure,* I was ready to hit the top-tier journals. I sent my primary work to the top of the top-tier general management journals the *Academy of Management Journal.* I was rejected, as AoM is above my level. Next, based on my area of study, small business and entrepreneurship, I decided to shoot for the top-tier journals in this niche. After about two years, I was published in the top-tier

Journal of Small Business Management, and I've continued at this level. This is actually above the level required at my school.

As far as conferences go, I've never sent a paper to the most prestigious AoM conference. I have published a few times at its Eastern Academy of Management conference, but I only send papers when it is local. The second most prestigious small business conference is USASBE, at which I have published, including winning the Coleman Foundation Best Empirical Paper award—plaque and $500. This is my level. However, I prefer the less prestigious third level Small Business Institute® conference. Some people attend both conferences. SBI papers meet the publishing requirements of my school. Another niche field I developed long after graduating is family business, which I will talk about in Chapter 6 as I explain how to multiple your publications.

Here is another example of finding your niche. At a university there is professor who was highly successful as a textbook writer. However, the school told him he needed refereed journal articles. His niche is not empirical or conceptual articles. However, textbook writing is very similar to writing informative articles. So the professor found the refereed journal *Business Horizons* that publishes his articles. Thus, he is meeting the publishing requirements of his school.

APPLICATION 3-2 (14)

What is my niche? How can I improve?

_____

_____

_____

_____

SELECTING TOPICS

Again, your focus should be on meeting your school publication requirements. Your niche provides you with a field of interest, but you need to be sure that the topic is publishable at the level you are seeking. Generally, the higher the level publication, the newer and greater the original contribution has to be. Here are some places to find and check on the worthiness of topics publication.

Ask Others, Editors and Special Issues

If you have topic ideas, or want to get ideas, you can check with others to make sure it is a good topic. People to ask are your mentors and reviewers, current and past professors, colleagues including doctoral friends and faculty members at your school and other schools.

Remember the tip from Chapter 2, write a proposal and have it reviewed. The publish ability of the topic at your desired level is an important part of the review. In fact, my tip is to check the topic as the first step because you don't want to write a proposal only to find out that the topic is not very likely to get published at your desired level.

Editors

Editors usually know what topics are hot. So to find out, you can contact editors and ask them if your topic is of interest and what other topics would be good to work on. I find that this approach is especially effective with editor-selected articles with a focus on informative how-to articles.

Editors of Selected Journals/Magazines

I've contacted a few of these editors and asked what topics of articles they are looking for. They rattle off a list. I select one of the topics, do a simple literature review, write the article, and send it in. I've never gotten a rejection. One journal, *Supervision*, paid me $50 for each article. I also had a few articles published in the American Management Association's *Supervisory Management*.

I worked on these publications in the early 1990s as a doctoral student to have some journal articles when I graduated.

However, several of the schools I was interested in apply to do not view these publications highly. So I focused on refereed journal articles. But your school may be pleased with this level publication, so go for it. It is fast and relatively easy.

If you explain to the editor that you would prefer a refereed article, and why, he or she may have it peer reviewed. Reviewers can be anyone the editor selects, and all it takes is one review to be refereed. If other academics have published in the journal, they would be idea reviewers.

Special Issue Call for Papers

As you read journals, keep an eye out for special issues. Based on the topic of the special issue, it can be a source of selecting a good topic and journal at the same time. There is often time to write an article for the special issue by the submission deadline.

Conferences

I recall the director of my doctoral program telling me that he had recently returned from a conference, and that the major reason he attended was to find out what the latest hot topics were in his field. He was holding a copy of the program listing all the papers as we spoke. Conferences tend to have a theme, and the theme is often a good topic for publication at the conference and in a journal article. Many researchers present papers on ideas they have for journal articles to follow.

Getting back to asking others, conferences are the perfect place to talk to others about topics. If you are new, don't be afraid to approach top-level publishers, this is an important benefit of conferences. You generally join and start out asking for help, and over the years in turn, you take the time to help others. Ask others if they think you have a good topic. If you like the paper presented, ask the author for recommendations on how you can extend the work on the topic. Conferences are also great places to find mentors and reviewers. You can try to get a few people to agree to review for each other.

Literature Search

After you have a topic idea, you should do a literature search on the topic to find out what has been published in this area. If you can't find any published articles within the last few years, maybe the topic is on the way down in publication interest. If your basic research question has already been answered, your article may be rejected for not meeting the so-what question: why is the topic important, why is there a need for your study-gap in the literature, what is the purpose of your study, and who can benefit from your work and how-implications? Refer to Chapter 9 for more details on the four parts needed to answer the so what question.

Further Research

As you most likely know, while doing your literature search, be sure to get copies of articles that you will include in your article's lit review. The tip here is to make sure you carefully read the discussion on the need for "further research" section. When you write your answer to the so what question, you want to back up your statements about the importance of your topic and need for your work with references based on the need for further research. Reference the discussion of the gap in the literature, and state how your work fills the gap—stating your contribution to the literature.

APPLICATION 2-1 (8)

How can I improve on selecting topics?

_____

_____

_____

_____

SELECTING PUBLICATION SOURCES

You only have so much time, so you have to carefully select the type of publication(s) you will work on. I can't overstate the importance of knowing and meeting your school's publishing requirements through your niche, and don't fool yourself into thinking you can replace publishing with other activities. Here are some pros and cons of each type of publication I introduced in Chapter 1. I'll give you more detailed tips on publishing in each source in Chapters 7 and 8.

Refereed Journal Articles

The reality is that the refereed journal article is generally given the most weight in evaluating your publishing record. Even if your school does not require them now, it could change the requirement and your ability to get tenure and promotions could be limited. If not required now, and you do publish articles, you should be a valued faculty member—a star. Also, if you are a professor and want to make a move to another school, without articles your mobility is very limited. The only thing you can take with you when you leave is your publication record.

The down side they are generally the most difficult to get accepted. There is the time and effort. It is not unusual to take two years to go from start to publication. Here is a review. For empirical articles, it often takes months to go through the process of selecting the topic, writing the proposal and having it reviewed, collecting and analyzing the data, writing, and proofreading the paper, having it pre-reviewed, revised, and proofread again before submitting for publication.

Once you submit it for publication consideration, depending upon the journal, it often takes two to three months before you get the publication decision. If rejected, you have to revise it and send it to another journal. As stated, I once did this 20 times. It is not common to get an accept as is; you usually have to revise and resubmit and wait another few months, only to find that another round of reviews is needed. I'll give you tips on handling the revise and resubmit in Chapter 7. Again, depending upon the journal, it could take up to a year before the article is actually published.

Conference Paper Proceedings.

Papers are generally given second status. They are generally easier to get accepted than articles and the start to finish time is much faster. A nice thing about conferences is that they have submission deadlines pushing you to get your paper done. The downside is that people often work on a paper that they know will be acceptable for a proceeding but will not be accepted by a journal. Thus, if journal articles are required and papers don't count much, time can be wasted. Recall the guy who fooled himself into thinking the school would count several proceedings as one journal article—he got fired. Below is a way to get both types of publications.

Papers to Articles

Conference papers are great because they give you the chance to multiply your publications as you improve your work. I recall my first Eastern Academy of Management conference and attending a presentation by a top-level author. He commented that his common practice, accepted by AoM and AACSB accreditation, was to work only on journal articles. He first presented the work at the regional conference to get reviews and revise the work to send to the national conference. After the national conference, he would revise the paper and submit it to a journal. I'll give you tips about this process in Chapter 6. The down side to this approach is the time.

When I have a good topic, sometimes I skip the conferences and go right to a journal. This is especially true when my pipeline is weak in the in-press stage. I'm constantly working to achieve my goal of two journal articles per year.

Editor-Selected Articles and Book Reviews

Editor-selected work is usually informative that is easier and much quicker to get published. I have a friend though SBI that is a book review editor for a journal. He called me and asked me to do a book review for him. I read the book and wrote the review in a week and it was published about a month later.

However, generally, editor-selected work doesn't help your publication record too much. If not, don't spend much time and effort working on this type of publication at the expense of proceedings and refereed journal articles. I actually did the book review as a favor, not really for the publication.

As there are always exceptions to my tips, if you are not able to publish at the higher level, or your school values this type of publication, go for it. I'll give you tips on publishing informative articles for practitioners and how to write book reviews in Chapter 8.

Authored and Edited Books/Textbooks and Chapters

Writing textbooks pay royalties, but they generally take a long time to complete and they are usually not given much weight in the evaluation process. Writing chapters in others books pays less and is usually of less value to your publishing record. With edited book you get other peoples work, you can make money, but again lower on the evaluation scale. In many fields, the number of textbook companies has shrunk and the competition has increased making it difficult to get a top level publisher.

A book that is not a textbook that actually contributes new knowledge to your field may have value on your publication record. But academic books don't usually sell that well, so income is often limited. My writing this book has taken time away from my article time.

I recall a professor from Northeastern University telling me that he asked his dean about writing a textbook. The dean's response was to focus on publishing refereed journal articles for career progression, and if you want to write a textbook do so as a business venture to make extra money. Think about it. It took me 1,700 hours (yes I actually log my time) to write my first textbook and instructor manual. I probably could have published 50 journal articles in that time. So for 1,700 hours I got one publication, not 50, on my CV.

My tip is again to know the requirements of your school and how much value you will get for writing a book. Ask your dean and chair if they recommend your writing a book. In most schools, I don't recommend trying to start with books, even if you can. After you have a publication record, then consider a book.

Textbook Supplements

We are going lower in the pecking order. Writing instructor manuals and test banks tend to pay a flat rate when given away free. They do tend to pay a royalty when sold as a separate supplement to the textbook—but many of today's students don't want to buy the textbook, never mind extras. If you do a good job, you don't make much on a per hour bases.

However, unless it is an acceptable method of meeting the publishing requirements of your school, and this is really your niche, I don't really recommend it myself. But I actually started my publishing career with textbook supplements, and I'll give you tips in Chapter 8.

Cases

Although listed last, depending upon the school publication requirements, based on the type of case and where it is published, cases may be given as high a status as refereed journal articles. A case based on primary data that is peer reviewed in a refereed case journal, or a journal that also has refereed cases, may be highly regarded. However, cases simply based on secondary data that are published in non-refereed books may be of little value.

Again, refereed journal articles are generally given the highest status. Some people you ask for advice about writing cases will tell you not to waste your time, others will advise you to write journal articles and that it's acceptable to write cases if you are interested, but not too many will suggest only writing cases. To conclude here, if you have a niche for publishing cases, check the school requirements to ensure their value and be sure to submit your cases to the right publications. I'll give you tips on writing cases in Chapter 7.

APPLICATION 3-4 (16)

Which type(s) of publication should I be working on? Am I spending enough time and effort on the most appropriate publication source? Should I cut back in some areas? How can I improve?

_____

_____

_____

FINDING THE APPROPRIATE JOURNAL

Your school requirements may give you a list of journals that you are expected to publish in, which is a big help if you can publish in these journals. However, there may not be a list and if you can't publish in the required or recommend journals, another part of your niche is to find journals that will publish your articles.

A common error is sending an article to a journal that is not a good fit, increasing rejection rates, not to mention wasted time and effort. I made this mistake by writing an informative article and sending it to a journal that published only short statistics-based empirical articles. The major reason this happened was because I didn't read the author guidelines to find out the details of what type of article the journal published.

Below are some methods of finding the right journal for your work. When searching for the right journal, be sure to strive for high quality prestige journals; more on quality in the next section. I have listed the methods in order of the most effective to the least effective. Regardless of how you find a journal, be sure to read the author guidelines.

Select the Journal Before Writing the Article

I actually select the journal before I write the article so that I'm sure to match the journal; we will discuss this in the next chapter, matching publication sources.

Follow the Reference Chain

Following the reference chain means that when you do your literature search, you get copies of the articles that are relevant to your study. From this group of articles, you look at the list of references and find others to get copies of and include in your lit review. Keep following the chain until you have copies of all the relevant articles related to your topic of study.

To find an appropriate journal, review each of the articles you have from your reference chain. Knowing your study and reviewing the articles from the various journals should give you a good idea if your article is a good fit for each journal. There may be multiple options, so keep quality in mind.

Ask Others, Conferences and Journals

Again, people to ask are your mentors and reviewers, current and past professors, colleagues including doctoral friends and faculty members at your school and other schools. If you followed the reference chain and have a few options, ask others for their advice on which journal to select.

Conferences

If you present a paper at a conference, take some of your presentation time to tell the audience that you are interested in revising your work and sending it to a journal. Ask them if anyone has a journal that would be interested in accepting the article. In addition, if you have options, again ask which one to select.

Journal Ads

As suggested, you should be reading journals in your field that are potential journals to publish in. Some journals publish ads for other journals, which is an indication that these journals may be looking for articles.

Journal Special Issues

Even though you already selected a topic and wrote an article, you may find a journal that is having a special issue, which is a great place to submit your article. But it has to be a good match.

Publication Listings

If you go to a database, such as Business Source Premier, LexisNexis Academic Universe, PsycINFO, and ERIC there should be a list of all the journals in the database. There may be hundreds, but you can go through the list looking for journal titles that sound like possible sources for your article. You can also search online journal listings, such as Emerald and Ingenta. There are also books that list hundreds of journals, such as *Cabell's Directory of Publication Opportunities in Business and Economics.*

Read Author Guidelines

Once you think you have selected a journal, keeping quality in mind, you are not done yet. Editors state that a high percentage of rejections are based on articles not being within the journal's objectives. So, although you think you have a match, you need to double check by reading the journal's author guidelines, which also have other names or parts like submission guidelines, mission statement and author guidelines, information for contributors, and so on. The guidelines are often in a hard copy of the journal, and they are virtually always found at the journal's website.

There are three important things to find out:

1. **Match**. The guidelines should include a statement (often called objectives, mission, purpose, journal overview) about the topics covered, articles (empirical, conceptual, informative, cases) it publishes, and sometimes making it clear what it doesn't publish, and length of articles. So if you don't have a good fit, keep searching for the right journal.

2. **So what question**. The guidelines often refer to the importance characteristics to get accepted, like making an original contribution and providing implications for practitioners. Knowing this, when you write your introduction and answer the so-what question, clearly state how you meet these publication criterion, your original contribution and/or implications required for publication. I actually tend to use the exact same wording from the guidelines. For example, the original contribution of this study is …. The implications for practitioners are ….

3. **Manuscript guidelines**. Be sure to follow the directions for formatting your article. Tips on this are in Chapter 4, Matching Publication Sources. With a good match, answering the so what question related to the objectives, and the proper format, you can send the article as directed. However, before submitting your article for publication, be sure to include the tips from the next chapter to complete the perfect match. An effective cover letter should also be written to the editor. Tips on cover letters are also in Chapter 4. Thus, you have another chapter of tips to increase your chances of getting

an acceptance before submitting your work for publication.

APPLICATION 3-5 (17)

How do I find journals? How can I improve?

_____

_____

_____

QUALITY VS. QUANTITY

It is nice to have only both high quality and quantity publications. However, not very many people can have both, especially novice researchers. Let's discuss what to strive for and how quality is determined.

Start with Quantity and Quality then Go for Quality

Let's start by repeating the need to meet the publication requirements of your school. If only top-quality journals listed count, you should still follow this tip as assurance that if you have to leave, you will have a publication record that is acceptable at another school.

It is hard to start at the top. So my tip is when you are starting, work up your acceptance rate building confidence and skill by starting with lower level quantity then go for quality. Start high, but again revise and resubmit to lower levels.

Don't Only Shoot for the Top

Recall that publishing is a numbers game. Here is my baseball game analogy followed by my academic rationale below: In baseball, if you go to the plate just trying to hit a home run, the odds are great that you will have a lot of strikeouts, and maybe no hits to show for your hard effort. If you go to plate just trying to get a hit, you may not get a home run, but you have something tangible for your effort.

I've known faculty who are hired and told the publication requirements. Let's say one refereed journal article every two years in a second or third tier journal. They come in with the attitude, "I'm going for the top tier journal." After three or four years, they don't have any articles yet. They keep fooling themselves into thinking, I can do it. But they don't. When they come up for tenure, all they can say is: "Give me more time and I will hit the big one." They may point to another colleague up for tenure and say that he has five articles, but they are all in third-tier journals. The response is, yes but he has five and gets tenure, and you have none and you don't get tenure—you perish.

If you have to leave without any refereed journal articles, it will most likely be hard to find another school that will hire you. With the next approach, even if you can't get the quality to get tenure, you will have some quantity to get another job with lower publication requirements.

Get Multiple Publications From Your Dissertation or Database—Shoot High and Lower at the Same Time

I'll give you tips on how to do this in Chapter 6, multiply your publications. Your dissertation should be able to get you at least a few articles. Take the best and send it to a high-level conference or journal that is a good match. At the same time, send your lower level quality articles from your dissertation to lower level journals to ensure you get some quantity. Once you have a foundation of publications, if you have great success with top tier journals, then you can focus only on that level.

Determining Quality

We all realize that the higher the quality articles you publish, or the better the journals, the higher the rated school that will hire you, and will usually pay you more. So the question is how do we know the quality of a journal? Here are some of the methods.

School Publication Requirements

The school grants tenure and promotions based on multiple criterion, one usually important criteria is publications. Whatever the school says is good enough quality, gets you tenure and promotion regardless of what other sources say.

However, you should publish at your level of ability. Be careful not to publish below your ability because publishing requirements can change. Besides, don't you want to be a star, rather than just a person the meets the minimum requirements? If for any reason you need or want to change schools, the higher the quality of your publications, the greater are your chances of getting another job.

Ask Others—Conferences

Again, ask others their opinion of the level of journals in your topic area. If you have two or more options to submit to, ask which of the journals they believe is the higher level? At a conference, you can also ask people how quality is determined at their school. If you get good ideas, you can try to change your school's rating system.

Rankings and Lists

If you do a search, you may find journal articles that give a ranking of journals. The Thomson Institute for Scientific Information (ISI) provides a listing of high-quality journals (scientific.thomson.com). It includes the Social Science Citation Index. If the journal is on the lists, it is considered a high quality journal.

Databases and Citation Source Lists

A journal that is listed usually has a higher rating than one that is not. The reason being, when people search the database for articles, they can find articles from that journal. Or, more people can find and read your article.

The Journal's Author Guidelines

Some journals will give you some of the information listed in the other sources of quality. For example, it may state the databases it is in, and it's ranking by some source.

APPLICATION 3-6 (18)

What is my balance of quality and quantity? How can I improve?

_____

_____

_____

SUMMARY OF TIPS

- Know the publishing requirements of your school.
- If you can't meet your schools publishing requirements, leave before you perish without tenure—leaving is not career failure.
- Don't fool yourself into thinking you can publish at a higher level than you are capable.
- Don't fool yourself into thinking other things (teaching, service) will take the place of publication requirements.
- Find your publishing niche.
- Ask others, including editors and people at conferences, for ideas on topics.
- Look for special issue topics.
- Conduct a literature search for topic ideas.
- When looking at articles on a topic of interest, be sure to pay close attention to the section on the need for further research to support your topic in answering the so-what question.

google this = spec. issue jour. educ-, etc.

- Select the publication sources to meet your school's publishing requirements, while using your abilities and preferences for the type of publications you want and can achieve.
- Follow the reference chain to find the right journal for your article.
- Ask others, including editors and people at conferences, where to submit your work for publication.
- Even after you have written an article, look for special issue topics that match yours.
- Find journals through publication listings, such as databases.
- Read the author guidelines to make sure your article matches the requirements of the journal.
- Start with quantity and quality, then go for quality; shoot high and lower at the same time.
- When selecting a publication source, determine the quality by knowing your school's publishing requirements.
- Other ways to determine the quality of a publication source are: asking others, ranking and lists, databases and citation source lists, and the journal author guidelines.

CHAPTER 4

MATCHING PUBLICATION SOURCES

CHAPTER OVERVIEW

In this chapter, the focus is on making sure that the topic and publication source you have selected do in fact match, which will increase your acceptance rate. I begin by stating two things editors and reviewers focus on.

- The second section explains the importance of reading the author guidelines and actual articles from the target publication source.
- Sections three and four give details of increasing the chances of getting the reviewers to believe you are a reader of the journal.
- The last section gives tips related to contacting editors.

CHAPTER OUTLINE

REVIEWER FOCUS

Before getting into matching publication sources, you should realize that whenever I use the word journal in this chapter, it can refer to both refereed and editor-selected journals and magazines, papers for proceedings and other sources of publications. However, there is more focus on matching journals.

Let's start with two things editors and reviewers are looking for in an article. First, they are looking for reasons to reject your work and they want articles from readers of the journal. Reviewers may not even be able to tell you they are looking for these two things because they often don't even realize it themselves, especially the first. Of course, there are always exceptions.

Reasons to Reject

First, remember that reviewers are not looking for reasons to accept your work; they look for reasons to reject it. This is part of the reason why rejection rates are so high. Therefore, you need to be sure that you don't give them reasons to reject your work, such as typos, spelling, English, and errors. As stated in Chapter 2, proofread carefully. However, even a well-written article that does not match the publication source will not lead to an acceptance. So the better you can match the publication's articles, the better are your chances of getting an acceptance.

Journal Reader

The second thing to remember is that reviewers typically want articles coming from its readers. Unless you are a reader of the journal, with the exception of big name authors, which blind reviewers don't know anyway, they are not really interested in giving you a publication. So you want to match the journal so well that even if you are not a regular reader of the journal the reviewers believe that you are.

Although you have selected a journal matching your article, as discussed in Chapter 3, there is still work to be done to ensure a perfect match. This chapter is all about matching the publication so well that it increases the odds of getting an acceptance, or to avoid rejection.

APPLICATION 4-1 (19)

Do I really understand what reviewers are looking for? How can I improve?

_____

_____

_____

READ AUTHOR GUIDELINES AND ARTICLES

As discussed in Chapter 3, you should read the author guidelines to make sure your article matches the journal. Now, you should read articles from the target journal, preferably related to your topic. If I don't already read and have copies of the journal and a few articles from the journal, I go to the Business Source Premier database and do an advanced search within the specific journal. You can also go to the journal's website and read the titles of all the articles published, as well as do a search for articles related to your topic. Either way, select some of the most relevant articles and get copies of them, if you don't already have them.

The next step is to read the articles. As you read, you might be able to do a quick read, examine the following to make sure your article is really a good match:

- *Introduction.* Read the introduction to see how the authors answered the so what question. Is your introduction's contribution at this level? If not, can you improve it to match?
- *Theory.* One of the big issues today with some of the high-level journals is developing a sound theory. So does your article develop a theory as well as the other articles? Is it based as the recent articles? If not, can you improve your theory building to match? This is one of my weaker areas.

- *Literature Review.* Is your literature review about the same length and level? If not, can you cut or add to it to improve your match?
- *Methodology.* Is your data collection, sample size, participants, and other methods at the level of the other articles? If not, you may not be able to change it, but you can also do another study matching the methods and statistics.
- *Statistics.* Is your statistical analysis at the same level? If the other articles ran regression, and you have t-test, you may not have a good match. Can you find someone who can help you with the statistics to get a better match?
- *Discussion/Implications.* Have you revisited your so what question and presented your discussion and the implications of your study at the same level as the other articles in the journal. If not, can you improve it to match?
- *Tables.* Do you have tables that provide the same information and statistical analysis as the other journals? If not, can you add tables, or improve yours to match?
- *References.* Do you have the same level of quality and quantity of references? If you have a lot more, you can cut some of the less relevant ones. If you have a lot fewer references, can you find more to improve your match?

It is time to do another assessment. Is your article a good match, or can you improve it to be a good match with the target journal? If not, you may want to find a better fit to improve your chances of getting accepted.

APPLICATION 4-2 (20)

Do I, or plan to, read author guidelines and articles from the targeted journal to ensure a good match? How can I improve?

_____

_____

_____

REFERENCE THE JOURNAL AND REVIEWERS

We have been focusing more on making sure you have a good match so you don't give the review any reason to reject your work. Now, let's address making sure that your article appears to come from a reader of the journal, even if you don't read the journal. Actually, if you have read some of the articles in the journal, you would be a reader of the journal. Get the editor and reviewer to believe you are a reader of their journal in three ways: reference articles from the journal, reference reviewers, and match the formatting exactly.

Reference Articles from the Journal Itself

If you already read some articles from your target match journal, it should be easy to add them to your article and the reference section. I was once told by someone at a conference that she had an editor of a journal make citing references from the journal a requirement for accepting the article. Would you protest?

I tend to shoot for around five references to be from the target journal. If I don't already have enough references, I do a search to find more articles to cite. I sometimes find good articles that I missed during the literature review that improve the article anyway. I've been known to stretch the relevance of a reference when I need to increase the number of citations by referencing very general comments that would be difficult to say are not stated or implied in the article.

Reference Reviewers of the Journal

This can be a tricky one, and you may not be able to do it, but it can help. Editors of the journal are also reviewers, so you can reference them too. Listing editors and reviewers as references actually gives them a reason to accept your article. Authors like having *citations*; their articles being referenced in other sources, especially high level journals. I referenced an editor once, and he was willing to accept my work and personally made changes to improve the article. I believe my citing him helped get the acceptance and his willingness to improve my article.

Also, I once got an "accept with minor revisions" decision on an article. One of the reviewers stated that I was missing some important references. He cited three articles that should be included in the article. Only one name was listed on all three articles, so I think I know who it was. But with a double-blind review, I can't be sure because someone else or a person only listed once could have been the reviewer, but really did believe they should be included. I believe this was an unethical way to get cited, but that is the editor's job to deal with. I simply included the references and got the publication.

Read the List of Reviewers

The journal itself, and the website, will include the editor(s) and a list of the reviewers of the journal. Read the list of names. Do you recognize any of the names as being experts in the topic area of your article? There is a good chance that this reviewer(s) will get your article. Do you already have an article they published from any journal? If so, be sure to include the name in your article and list of references.

Do an Author Name Search

If you do recognize a reviewer as being an expert in your topic, but don't have a reference or you want more references, do a database search using the author's name. Try to select at least one article and cite it in your article and list of references.

Matching Helps, No Guarantees

Obviously, referencing articles from the journal and referencing reviewers, and using the exact format, will only help if you really have a good match to the journal. They are the type of things that can take a borderline article into the acceptance pile by not proving any reasons to reject the article. The third method of getting reviewers to believe you are a reader of their journal is to match the formatting exactly; these tips are covered in the next section.

APPLICATION 4-3 (21)

Do I, or plan to, reference articles for the target journal and reference reviewers? How can I improve?

_____

_____

_____

_____

EXACT FORMATTING

Although it takes some time, I personally make sure that the format of my paper or article is the exact same as the target proceedings or journal. To match formatting, I have a copy of journal/proceedings or at least one article and the author guidelines (directions) in hand. A good secretary or student aide can do this for you.

Recall that I suggested selecting the journal before actually writing the article. In doing so, you set up the format exactly as you write it, rather than having to go back and change it. Here are the things I make sure to match with the journal.

- *Title.* I make the title around the same length as the articles in the journal. I notice that many of the journals I send to have sub-titles, like Success versus Failure: An International Comparison. I make the size of the font and CAPS or not to match.
- *Headings, margins, fonts.* I match the heading as CAPS or not, center or left justified, left or justified text, size of font, and so on as commonly stated in the author guidelines and visible in the articles.
- *References citations in article.* In my field of management, many of the journals claim to use APA style, but what they really mean is having the author and year of publication

like Lussier and Smith (2009). But in reality, many of the journals use different formats. This is a common one that changes among journals:

(Lussier, Jones and Smith 2009)
(Lussier & Smith 2009)
(Lussier, Jones, & Smith, 2009).

Notice the change in using the word "and vs. &" and the use of a comma between authors and year.

- *Hypotheses and Tables.* I've noticed a lot of variation in format of hypotheses. Some are italic, some use the full word hypothesis and others only H1, H2, some are indented. Table headings can be on one line or two, some are CAPs, and others are bold.

- *Reference List.* Reference formatting can be different, so I do take the time to do an exact match. Here are two examples:

Lussier, R. N. and Jones, K. (2009). Success vs. failure in retailing. *Journal of Small Business Strategy 19,* 2, 132–46.
Lussier, R. N. & K. Jones (2009). "Success vs. Failure in Retailing," *Journal of Small Business Strategy 19*(2): 132–146.

Many people consider following author guideline directions and matching format as minor and question if it is worth the time and effort. Let me ask you a question. Do you have students write papers that are supposed to be done according to your directions? Let's say your directions are to double space and the paper is single spaced. When you get a paper not following directions, what is your first impression? Does this impression affect your attitude toward the paper and grade? I actually take off points for not following directions.

I can tell you that editors and reviewers are readers of the journal and will notice if you don't follow their journal's format. Again, reviewers are looking for reasons to reject your paper. Do you want to give reviewers a reason to reject your work? If you have a borderline revisable paper, you could get a reject for not following author guidelines. I had an editor send me back an article telling me to format correctly.

Being persistent means revising and re-submitting. One of the things that irritate me is getting a rejection. I have to select another journal to send my article to. Now, I don't only have to make revisions to the content based on review comments, I also have to go through the entire paper and reformat to match the new journal. Again, a good secretary or student aide can do this for you.

APPLICATION 4-4 (22)

Do I, or plan to, carefully follow author guidelines and match articles exactly? How can I improve?

BE A REVIEWER

This tip, be a conference proceedings and/or journal reviewer, has some negatives and positives. On the negative side, it takes time to review other peoples' work that you could be spending on your own publishing work.

Benefits

On the positive side, you do get service experience for being a reviewer that you can list on your CV and for tenure and promotion. You also get a feel for the other side and how others may be viewing your work, and get ideas of what to do and not to do when writing articles.

Politics

A major advantage is playing politics. If you are a reviewer and you do a good job, you can develop a relationship with the editor (or people making paper decisions for conferences), especially if the editor asks for a favor, like a quick turnaround.

Based on your working relationship, when you send in an article the editor may be more inclined to send your article to reviewers known to be higher on recommending acceptances. Also, if there is a split decision among reviewers, the editor may tend to give a revise and resubmit to a good reviewer that might get a rejection.

My Politics

I did play politics at least twice. I had a friend who wanted me to go to a conference, but I said the deadline for papers has past and I can't get funding to go without presenting. He said, give me a paper; I think I can get you in. My friend was a friend of the person making the paper decisions, so he called the VP of programs and asked him what he could do. My paper was accepted and I presented. Also, I was VP of programs and after the paper deadline I remembered that one of my mentorees hadn't sent in a paper. I contacted him and told him to get it in; then I got another coauthor friend to do a quick review in time to get into the proceedings and come to the conference.

Helping Others

I actually didn't start reviewing for several years, and I review more for giving back as service to my profession than any other reason. I was asked to be a reviewer by two journal editors. But you can volunteer. Many conference track chairs ask for volunteers to review, and many take anyone. Reviewing for a journal is more selective. You can volunteer, but the editor will generally expect that you have published in the journal, or in other journals of the same level or higher.

APPLICATION 4-5 (23)

Am I, or plan to be, a reviewer? How can I improve?

_____

_____

_____

CONTACT EDITORS, REVIEWER FORMS AND COVER LETTERS

There are three primary reasons to contact the editor. First, if you are not sure you have a good match and another is to get copies of reviewer forms. Once you have a good match based on everything in the last chapter and everything in this chapter, you should submit your article with a well written cover letter.

Determining Match

So far I assumed that you found a match for your article. So you may be thinking, what if I'm not sure it is a good match? Before going through the rest of the tips in this chapter to match the publication source, you can find out if you have a good match by contacting the editor of the journal and asking. Explain your article and ask if the editor would be interested in reviewing the manuscript for possible publication.

Get Referrals
If the editor is not interested in your work, ask if he or she knows of a journal that would be interested in your article. Getting back to selecting topics, Chapter 3, contacting the editor works especially well with editor selected journals/magazines.

Get Reviewer Forms

Even if you believe you have a good match, there is one good reason to contact the editor—to get copies of reviewer forms. Today with the push for student outcomes and assessment, there is a call for more grading rubrics so that students know how their work is evaluated. The same should hold true for journal articles. Editors give reviewers grading rubrics to complete.

It is helpful to know how your article will be assessed by the reviewers. Journals generally send out a copy of the article with the reviewer form to be completed for each reviewer, but authors don't get copies until after the review. You can contact editors informing them that you will be submitting an article and ask them for a copy of the reviewer form to aid you in matching the journal requirements.

With the reviewer form, rate your own article. Also, it is a good idea to give a copy of the reviewer form to the people who will pre-review your article before sending it in to the journal for review. The reviewer form will help the pre-review focus on the important aspects with suggestions for improvement. Refer back to Chapter 2 for the discussion on getting pre-reviewers.

Cover Letters to Editors

Many journal editors reject a very high percentage of manuscripts. Some editors reject more than 90%, and recall that the majority of rejections are due to not being a good match for the journal. So in your cover letter you want to convince the editor that your article really is a good match. Getting the editor interested in publishing your manuscript may help in reviewer selection and into the revise and resubmit stage. The cover letter/e-mail to the editor is a method that can get the interest of the editor. Thus, take the time to write a good cover letter.

In the cover letter/e-mail to the editor of the journal introducing your manuscript, be sure to state the fit to the journal's mission. Important questions to focus on are: Why should the editor publish your article? Why would the readers of the journal want to have your article included in the journal? Why would a person doing a search of your topic want to read your article? In essence, you are including a "brief answer" to the so-what question (Chapters 2 and 3—why is the topic important, what is the need for your research-lit gap, what is the purpose of the research-original contribution, and what are the implications?), which you should already have in your introduction, but with a clear focus on answers to the new three questions stated.

APPLICATION 4-6 (24)

Have I ever contacted an editor to ask about fit and/or for a reviewer form? Do I write good cover letters? Should I? How can I improve?

_____

_____

_____

SUMMARY OF TIPS

- Remember that reviewers are really looking for reasons to reject your work, not for reasons to accept it. So don't give them reasons to reject.
- Remember that reviewers want articles from readers of the journal, so don't let them think you are not a reader.
- Remember that the majority of articles are rejected because they are not a good match to the journal criterion, so be sure you have a match.
- Read the author guidelines to make sure your work meets the publication criterion of the target journal.
- Read some articles from the target journal to make sure you have a good match.
- Reference the target journal by doing a literature review of the journal to find articles to cite in your work and list in the reference section.
- Reference reviewers of the target journal.
- Match the formatting of the author guidelines and articles: title, headings, margins, fonts, reference citations in article, hypotheses, tables, and reference lists.
- Be a reviewer.
- If you are not sure you have a match, contact the editor and ask.

- Get copies of reviewer forms to understand publication criterion and if you have a match.
- Send a cover letter with your article briefly answering the so what question

CHAPTER 5

TIME MANAGEMENT

CHAPTER OVERVIEW

This chapter is designed to help you better manage your time so you can publish.

- In the first section, you determine your priorities.
- Section two asks you how much time do you actually spend working on publishing, and suggests keeping a log to find out for sure.
- The third section suggests teaching fewer courses, if possible, and teaching multiple section of the same course to cut down on prep time, so you have more publishing time.
- Section four presents possible class schedules to help you find the time to publish, it suggest that you set a publishing schedule, and that you keep to your publishing schedule just like you do with your teaching schedule.
- The fifth section discusses using a home vs. school office for publishing.
- Section six gives you tips on using student, and other, assistants.
- The last section provides several ideas to help you manage your time.

CHAPTER OUTLINE

PRIORITIZING PUBLISHING

In this opening section, you will learn about your publishing priority, the difference between important and urgent things to do, and what to do if you are too busy to get to your priority of publishing.

Your Publishing Priority

Let's begin by determining what your priority is for publishing. The first thing I'd like you to do right now before reading on is to state what type of priority publishing really is for you and your career. Now determine your priority based on the three general categories of tenure and promotion:

1.   Teaching is more important to me and my career.
2.   Publishing is more important to me and my career.
3.   Service to the college and profession is more important to me and my career.
4.   Or they are all equally.

If not equal, rank them from high to low priority. Also, put a percentage that determines the importance of each to you and your career, to equal 100 percent. For example, teaching 50%, publishing 40%, and service 10%.

My Priority Ranking	Percentage
1.	
2.	
3.	

Your School's Priorities
Now that you answered what your top priority is, when it comes to tenure and promotion at your school, is teaching, publishing, or service given more weight or are they equal? If

not, what is the school's ranking? Is your answer really correct? Think about it.

Many schools say teaching, publishing, and service are equal, but when it comes down to the decision, teaching is often subjective and either you are acceptable or not (and this is usually determined in the first couple of years, because if you aren't acceptable you are out), but publishing has clearer objective measures that are often really given more weight at the time of tenure and promotion. As stated, you can be the best teacher and not get tenure and promotions. At many schools, service is really not all that important, and is measured subjectively as either acceptable or not. Now that you have had some time to think about it, what are your school's "real" priorities? Again, rank the three from high to low with percentages.

School-Weighted Ranking	Percentage
1.	
2.	
3.	

Do your Priorities Match Your School's Priorities?

If not, should you change your priorities? Another option to changing your priorities is to get a job at a school with a better match to your priorities. Let's face it; you will generally be much happier at a school that has the same priorities as you do. But this can't always happen. I'm at a school that has a lower publication priority than I do, and it has caused some friction, disappointment, and frustration. Associating with a lot of great people in the SBI® and having co-authors from other schools has really helped me to associate with people at my publication level, which is very satisfying.

Publishing Attitude

Let's get back to attitude towards publishing (Chapter 1). Often there is a relationship between attitude toward publishing and the prioritization of publication. Do you have a match in attitude (positive or negative) and priority (1–3) towards publishing? If publishing is important to your school and not a high priority for you, maybe an attitude adjustment can help, as suggested in Chapter 1. Associating with people who do publish, and working with them, can also help. We will discuss co-authors in Chapter 6.

Important vs. Urgent Priorities

One of the things about publishing journal articles is that it is always considered an important priority, but it usually isn't urgent. Therefore, people tend to do the less important things that seem to be urgent, and they don't put in the time to do the important things—publishing. One good thing about publishing papers in proceedings is that the call for papers has a due date. Thus, the due date makes finishing the paper urgent as it comes close, pushing academics to get the work done. One tip on journal articles is to set a deadline for submission; write it down and meet your deadline.

Don't Be Too Busy to Publish

When I conduct workshops and ask participants if they are putting in enough time working on publishing, they commonly say they are too busy. My response is that if publishing is really a priority, you have to cut back on other activities that are less important and put the time into publishing. Here are a few ideas.

Grants
If you get a government, or any organizational, grant, the grant money typically will pay for you to get out of some of your teaching during the year so that you can have time to do research, and it provides you with some extra income as well. Your school may have a grants office, or people, who can help you apply for grants.

Don't Teach Summers

One tip here is not to teach in the summer; put in the time working on increasing your publishing productivity. If you say you can't afford not to teach summers, my response is: Can you afford to lose your job or not get a promotion and raise?

School Summer Grants

Also, many schools have some form of research grants that allow you to do scholarly work, with pay, during the summer. I'm currently working on a proposal for this coming summer. If your school doesn't have a summer grants program, you can try to get the school to start one.

The rest of this chapter will give you tips to help you manage your time better so that you will get your publishing time-in, our next topic.

APPLICATION 5-1 (25)

Is there a match between my priorities and the school's tenure and promotion evaluation requirements? Do I get my publishing done? How can I improve?

_____

_____

_____

_____

TIME-IN AND LOG-IN YOUR TIME

Time-in refers to how much time you actually spend working on publishing. Log-in your publishing time is a listing of how many hours per week you actually do work on publishing.

Time-in Publishing

To determine time-in publishing, let's focus on answering some questions. The questions are often a rude awakening for academics. During the semester and between semesters and during the summer, how many hours per week on average do you actually spend working on publishing?

Hours per week working on publications during the semester	
Hours per week working on publications between semesters and summers	
During the semester, how many hours per week on average do you spend on teaching and service activities?	
Hours per week working on teaching activities	
Hours per week working on service activities	

Does Your Priority Percentage Match the Time You Put Into Teaching, Publishing, and Service?

There is usually a direct relationship between time-in working on publishing and the number of publications. If you stated that publishing was a 30 percent priority for you and your school, do you put in 30 percent of your time working on publications? Is it at least close?

My priority is 45% for both teaching and publishing and 10% for service. As a textbook author, on average, during the semester I work about 20 hours on teaching (four courses per semester), 20 hours on publishing, and 2 hours on service. Between semesters and during the summer, all but a few weeks a year, I put in 40 hours per week working on publishing. Summer is a prime time for me to work on textbooks, but I work on proceedings, journal articles, and textbooks all year long. I publish at a much higher level than my school requirements.

Based on your school's tenure and promotion evaluation system:

Is your time spent properly balanced in teaching, publishing, and service?	
Are you putting in enough time to accomplish your publishing priority?	

Are you on track to meet the publishing requirements of your school?	
How many hours per week should you be working on publishing?	

Log-in Publishing Time

Many people misjudge how much time-in publishing they really complete. The only way to really be sure how much time you put in publishing is to log-in your time, as I do. My tip is for you to do the same. I have a calendar on my desk and when I sit down to work on publications, I write down the time I start and stop (rounding off to the nearest 15 minutes); I don't count breaks, lunch, or necessary interruptions. I total the hours each week. So when I listed 20 and 40 hours per week, I'm not guessing. My mentorees have told me that log-in time and scheduling publishing time (to be discussed in this chapter) really helps them stay at their target number of hours per week to publish.

Actually, the rest of this chapter is full of tips that can help you to improve your time academic management skills. You can increase your publishing productivity with techniques that have helped me to have a successful publishing career, and others who have given me some of the tips.

APPLICATION 5-2 (26)

Go back and review the questions and tips above. What can I cut back on to improve my time-in? Will I use a log to determine how much time I actually do spend on publishing?

_____

_____

_____

_____

TEACHING PREPS

Many schools give you the option of selecting the courses you will teach, so in this section I present tips on a way to teach less and to select teaching preps to save time for publishing. What I'm getting at here is to work at keeping the number of courses you teach and the amount of time you need to prepare to teach your classes to a minimum so that you will have time to work on publications. I already stated that getting grants may allow you to teach less.

You probably already know the courses that are your stronger areas that will require less class preparation time. But have you given any thought to the number of different courses you will teach? The fewer the courses and the number of different courses you teach, the less time you will need to prepare for classes, and the more time you will have to publish. Here are two tips:

Reassigned Time

Many schools with a larger teaching load (four courses per semester) give faculty reassigned time to work on scholarly publications, usually one course release for the semester. If reassigned time is available, take the time to apply for it to cut down your teaching load. If your school doesn't have reassigned time, or enough awards, you can try to get the school to offer reassigned time, or to provide more awards. My school does offer a limited number, and I have applied and received reassigned time.

Teaching Multiple Sections

Another way to cut back on teaching prep time is to teach multiples sections of the same course, rather than different courses, if you can. Over 30 years, I have always taught as many sections of Principles of Management as I can, between two and three. I currently teach four courses per semester including three sections of Management and one section of Corporate Social Responsibility. I have the same schedule both semesters. Teaching the same courses year after year results in less preparation. Plus, I use my own textbooks, so I have very little preparation to do for class.

APPLICATION 5-3 (27)

Do I opt to teach less and to teach multiple sections? How can I improve?

SCHEDULING CLASSES AND PUBLISHING TIME

Here I give tips on when to schedule your classes. Also, I actually suggest scheduling time to publish and treating class and publishing schedules the same.

Scheduling Classes

Many schools give faculty input into when they will teach their courses. When you teach has a direct relationship with publishing productivity. If you haven't figured it out yet, to be successful at publishing generally takes large blocks of time. Many of us can't get much done in one or two hours between classes and during office hours. For one thing, there are too many interruptions from faculty and students. About the only things I do for publishing between classes and during office hours is to run statistics and once in a while I will do some proofread.

Publishing Days—No Teaching

If possible, have days that you don't have to teach so that you can get in large blocks of time to focus solely on publishing. I currently teach on Tuesday and Thursday and have office hours going from 8–4. On Wednesday nights, I do 6:30–9:30. This gives me three full days to work on publishing without having to write nights and weekends.

Teach Nights

If you teach at night, you can have all day to work on publishing. I don't have to teach on Wednesday night; I want the day time to write. One of my colleagues teaches three nights a week so that he has all day to work on publishing.

Work on Publishing ½ the Day—Avoid Mid-Day Classes

What tends to happen when you have mid-day classes is you tell yourself you don't have time to work on publishing in the morning before classes and then after classes you are too tired or find some other reason not to work on publications.

When I had to teach five days a week, I tried two different schedules. Sometimes I'd write in the mornings and teach afternoons or nights. Other times I'd schedule morning classes and then spend the afternoon working on publishing.

Write During Your Prime Time

I found that I was more productive writing before classes, as I was a bit tired and distracted after teaching. So another tip is to work on publishing when you are at your best—prime time. Some people are at their best at night. When are you most productive working on publications?

Scheduling Publishing Time

If you have come up with a number of hours you want to work on publishing each week, the next step is to schedule the time. The log-in publishing time approach can be done during your scheduled publishing time to keep a record of your hours over time. Use the log if you want to know how many total hours it took you to complete an article or book.

Scheduling time to publish is one thing most people haven't thought of doing, and not too many people actually do it, but a BIG tip is to schedule time to work on publishing. Right now it may be too late to schedule your classes, but it isn't too late to schedule time to publish. If you have a scheduled time to work on publications, you can go on to the next part of this section, treating teaching and publishing schedules the same.

People who will not commit to a publishing schedule tend to take the old "I'll publish when I get around to it." The problem is that they never seem to get around to it, because they are too busy doing urgent things that are not really important, so they don't have a successful publishing career. If you say you are too busy to find time to publish, here are more options of how other busy people that give publishing a high priority find time to write.

Work at Least 40 Hours Per Week

I remember a colleague once stating that he didn't think there were very many faculty members who actually put in a 40 hour week. Do you? When I say work, I mean actual working time—not including socializing, breaks, and meals. How many hours per week do you spend talking to colleagues without getting any work done? I'm not saying to be antisocial, but don't count this time as working. Office hours, part of teaching time, are a great time to socialize. If you were in business making the salary paid at a good university, you would most likely be working 50–60 hours per week. So if you don't actually work 40 hours a week, increase your publishing time.

Write at Night

Some busy people with child care responsibility during the day will write at night when the kids are sleeping. I know a guy who was very busy with young children and he had to teach four courses per semester. How he fit in his publishing time was to go to bed at around 9 after getting his kids to bed. He would get up at 1 am and work on publications until 4 am then he went back to bed. He was up at 6 getting his kids ready for their day.

Write Early Morning

I know people who get up at 3–4–5 am five days a week to work on publishing before they get their kids up and go teach. Some simply start this early because it is their prime time. If you start working on publications this early, then mid-day classes are fine because you already spent half your work day publishing.

Write on Weekends

Yes. I know you don't want to work on weekends, but if you can't find any other time, do it. Although not scheduled, I've already spent one Saturday and Monday holiday working on this book.

Most people don't really want to spend time on nights and weekends working. But if publishing is really a priority, and you can't fit it in during the week days, then to be successful at publishing you have no other options that I can think of. Is it worth giving up 3–4 hours once or more times a week to increase your publishing productivity? If not, publishing is NOT a priority for you. So the question is: What days and times are you scheduling to work on publications?

Treating Teaching and Publishing Schedules the Same

Most faculty members are very good about their teaching schedule; they show up to all their classes, they are on time, and conduct class for close to the full scheduled time. However, many people who schedule time to work on publishing don't keep to their publishing schedules; they skip the publishing time, start late, and stop early.

Question Cutting Publishing Time

Treating teaching and publishing schedules the same can help you to keep to your schedule. Here is how you do it. Do not skip or cut a publishing session short for any reason that you would not skip or cut class time. Anytime you have something to do, ask yourself this question. Would I skip or cut class short to do this thing? If not, keep to your publishing time. For example, if a friend called and asked you to get together for lunch during a class time, would you cut class? If not, why should you cut publishing time? Do you answer your phone and check voice and e-mail messages during class? If not, why should you during your publishing time? Find another time.

Make Up Missed Publishing Time

Yes. There are times when you will have to miss or cut your publishing time. However, if you do, schedule a make-up session. The make-up usually has to be done at night or on weekends, when most people don't want to work. If you force yourself to make up the time during hours you don't want to work, you will be surprised at how well you keep to your scheduled publishing time.

APPLICATION 5-4 (28)

What will my future class schedule be? What is my publishing schedule? Will I make up any missed scheduled time for publishing? How can I improve?

_____

_____

_____

_____

WHERE TO WORK ON PUBLISHING

So you have decided that publishing is a priority, you know how many hours per week you want to work at publishing, and you have a schedule. So now, where should you write? I'll give you my biased view of publishing at home, followed by tips for writing at school for those who prefer to be away from home.

My basic approach is when I'm in my school office I work on teaching and service, mostly department service work. When

I'm home during the day, I work on publishing in my home office. So essentially, on Monday, Wednesday, and Friday during the day I work on publishing at home (20 hours a week). All day Tuesday and Thursday and Wednesday night I'm working on teaching and service at school (20 hours a week).

Home Office

Here are reasons why I work on publishing in my home office.

- *Fewer interruptions.* I work best when I can totally focus on my publication. At school there are too many interruptions. Other professors and students will walk in and talk to me about irrelevant things, which is fine during my office hours. If I'm in my office, the administrative assistant will send students with questions to see me even if it has nothing to do with me. I'll tell you how I deal with interruptions at home below.
- *Comfort.* When I'm on campus, I'm dressed in business casual clothes. I'm more comfortable in shorts and sweats. I'm also more comfortable in my home office, which is much nicer.
- *Stress.* I feel more stressed at school. I tend to want to leave to go to my home office, so I find myself pushing to finish.
- *Breaks.* When I want to take a short break, there is nothing for me to do at school, besides going to talk to other faculty and taking up their time. I'd rather socialize during my school time. At home I can relaxingly take five, ten to fifteen minutes to putter around the house or use my own bathroom.
- *Lunch.* I also don't really want to go to lunch at the all-you-can-eat diner and pig out and gain weight. Eating in my office or office area is not relaxing. I much prefer to make my own lunch at home.
- *Taxes.* As a textbook writer, I have royalty income. Therefore, I claim a home office as an expense on my income taxes Schedule C—Profit or Loss from Business. As long as

you have income (book royalties, consulting fees, speaking/tutoring income, etc.), you may be able to claim a home office expense to offset some, or all, of your taxable income. But don't say I told you that you can. Check with a tax expert to see if you quality, like I did.

- *Legal issue.* Also, although it is hard to believe and you can't believe your school would do this to you, I heard that there is a potential legal case for writing books in your school office. In the state of Massachusetts, a college professor used his school office to write a textbook. The school asked for a share of the royalties. When the professor refused, the college took him to court and won. The professor wrote the next edition of the textbook at home. No, it wasn't me.

Dealing with Personal Interruptions at Home

One of the difficult parts of working on publications at home is personal interruption by spouses/significant others and children. How I cut this way down was to talk to my wife about it a few times telling her that although I'm in the house, I'm in my home office working. If I were at school, would you come to talk to me about this issue or call me? If it would wait until I'm home, then let it wait until I'm finished by scheduled publishing time.

- *Home office hours.* Telling your household members what your scheduled publishing hours are really helps. If they know the hours not to bother you, then it is easier to wait until your hours are over.
- *Home office with a door and your own computer.* Having an actual place you call your home office with a door you can shut and your own computer to work on helps to define where you want to be alone to work and the other places are where to talk. At night, I check my personal emails, and those related to publishing, in my home office, but I keep the door open so others can talk to me. The room can be multifunctional, like a spare bedroom, but call it

your home office. If I could only have part of another room, I'd try to set some type of boundaries and still call my area my office.

- *Home office isolation.* A good place to have a home office is away from high activity rooms, often the kitchen and living room. Up and down stairs and the ends of the house away from the activity rooms make it harder to get to you to talk.

School Office

I know. Some of you are saying I can't work at home because I don't have the discipline to just work on publications. There are too many distractions or interruptions at home. If you are not productive at home, here are a few tips.

- *Isolation.* Have your school office in an isolated area.
- *Closed door.* Close your office door to avoid interruptions.
- *Don't answer the phone/text or check emails*—this goes for home office too. You can end up stopping your important publication time for less important urgent things that can really wait. Deal with phone and email issues during office hours, not publishing hours.

- *Quite.* Schedule your publishing time during quite office hours, often early and late.
- *Other location.* Consider some other location, such as some other office on campus or the library.

APPLICATION 5-5 (29)

Where will I work on publications? How can I improve?

_____

_____

_____

_____

Student Assistants

In this section, I'll present a time management techniques that can cut back on your teaching time to give you more time to spend on publishing. Although the heading states student assistance, you may also be able to use administrative and other assistance. I once asked a dean for some help, and she had one of her office staff work on a project for me. I know a guy who is really only as good as the assistance that he get from others.

Having your own graduate student assistant is your best option. If you can get one, do so. If not, maybe you can share one. If not, maybe you can get an undergrad student aide. The potential problems with undergrads are their ability to be helpful due to lack of experience and the potential restrictions on what they can do.

Some schools do not allow undergrads to have any access to seeing other students' grades. Some allow it after students sign a confidentiality agreement. I suggest following the school policies and rules of student use. I've had some excellent undergrad help.

You may be thinking, everyone knows you should use assistants, so here are some things that student and other assistants can do. There are two categories of assistance given here: teaching and publishing. However, assistants are also great help when it comes to service. I know SBI® officers who have their assistants do much of the work for them.

Assistance with Teaching

Here are some tips related to teaching activities. Have an assistant:

- *Grade book.* Set up your grade book, such as type or write in student names.
- *Correct and grade papers and exams.* This saves me a lot of time.

- *Enter grades.* Even if you do your own grading, at least let an assistant put the grades in your grade book.
- *Type things.* For example, I have students do presentations and the assistant types the 60 student names that are presenting.
- *Copies.* Make copies, or bring them to and from your office for copying.
- *Errands.* Run errands around campus, like hand delivering important papers (your contract, application for tenure, etc.)
- *Give your exams.* By not having to go to class, you may be able to stay home and work on publishing all day.
- *Conduct a few classes for you.* Again, you may work on publishing instead of going to class.
- *Cover a class you can't attend.* One of my written assignments is completing a resume. So when I go away to a conference and miss class, I have a person from the career center come to my class and discuss what the career center has to offer and go over how to write a resume.

Assistance with Publishing

Here are some tips related to publishing activities. Have an assistant:

- *Literature.* Do a literature search for you.
- *Copies.* Get copies of specific articles you want to read.
- *Collect data.* For example, working on a mail questionnaire. My co-author, Matthew Sonfield from Hofstra University, had an assistant go through copies of a journal and get the names and e-mail addresses of all the foreign authors so we could contact them.
- *Data entry.* Enter data into your statistical software, or other source. Sonfield's assistant typed up the e-mail list to send his letter.
- *Run statistics.* Run statistics for you and give you the printouts.

- *Select statistics.* A quality person can even help you determine which statistics to run and interpret the statistical printouts. I have a research methods and stats teacher at Springfield College, Krista Winter, whom I occasionally check with. When working on my research methods and statistics for business book with Waveland Press, she was helpful answering some questions I had.
- *Type numbers.* Type in the numbers from the statistical printout into your tables.
- *Type references.* Type the reference list from your actual abstracts and articles.
- *Edit.* Edit your article to match the formatting of the target journal (Chapter 4).
- *Proofread.* Proofread your paper or article (Chapter 1) at various stages.
- *Review.* A quality person (doctoral student) may even be a reviewer of your proposals and articles (Chapter 2). Even if you don't have a doctoral program in your department or school, you may be able to get one from another one. When I was working on my dissertation, back when using SPSS was complicated needing codes, I asked the research and statistics expert about help and she had her physical education doctoral grad assistant help me.

APPLICATION 5-6 (30)

Do I, or plan to, use student and other assistants? What will I have them do? How can I improve?

_____

_____

_____

_____

GENERAL TIME MANAGEMENT TIPS

As stated in the heading, here are some general time management tips. They are adapted from my *Management Fundamentals: Concepts, Applications, Skill Development* 4th ed. (South-Western/Cengage, 2009, pp. 160–162).

- *Distractions.* Remove all non-publication related and distracting objects from your work area/desk—*cell phone off and out of site.*
- *Don't answer the phone/text or check e-mails* during publishing time. Deal with them during office hours, not publishing hours. The exception here would be if it is publishing related. For example, during a short break from publishing, I will check my e-mail to see if a co-author or editor has contacted me, especially if I'm waiting for a response. However, I don't check any personal e-mails until after publishing time is over, usually at night after supper.
- *Interruptions.* Try to avoid interruptions, but when you are interrupted, before you stop working on publishing to do another task, *ask yourself. Is this task really more important than publishing,* can it wait until my scheduled publishing time is over?
- *Set a deadline* for each publication. Be sure to include time to have your work pre-reviewed. Be careful not to underestimate the time it takes to complete a publication. A general guide is to estimate the time, then double it.
- *Set earlier deadlines* than the actual deadline to give you a cushion if you need it and to make sure you have it proofread.
- *Break the publication work into parts* to keep from being overwhelmed. With an article, just focus on one part at a time. With a book, focus on one chapter and each section of a chapter at a time.
- *Objective.* Have a clear *objective* for each publishing session. Today I will: do a literature search, collect data, run statistics, write the introduction/results section, etc.

- *Don't procrastinate,* do it.
- *Don't spend time performing unproductive activities* to avoid or escape anxiety. It doesn't really work; get working on your publications, get it done, and you will feel much better.
- *Keep a clean, well-organized work area/desk.* But don't waste your publishing time cleaning up.
- *Do take the time to train assistants;* don't do the things others can do for you.
- *Do take some breaks,* but do get back to work. Getting too tired tends to lead to mistakes. Short physical activity for 5–10 minutes is a great way to invigorate yourself— stretch, take a quick walk, do some jumping jacks.
- *Time savers.* Consistently try to combine and modify activities to save time.

APPLICATION 5-7 (31)

Which tips can help me improve my time management?

_____

_____

_____

_____

SUMMARY OF TIPS

- Determine your teaching, publishing, and service priorities ranking and percentages.
- Determine your school's priorities.
- Determine if your priorities match your schools, and if you should change yours.
- Do your important publishing rather than the urgent priorities.
- If you are busy, get grants, don't teach summers, and get summer grants from your school.

- Determine how many hours per week that you actually put into working on publications and how many hours you should be working—goal.
- Log-in your publishing time to determine if you are working as many hours as you should be, and to motivate you to meet your average weekly goal.
- Cut your teaching time through grants, release time, and other methods.
- Cut your teaching preparation time by teaching multiple sections.
- Schedule your classes to allow blocks of time to publish—no teaching days, teach nights, teach ½ days—avoid mid-day classes—and publish ½ days, and write during your prime time.
- Do schedule time to publish each week.
- Too busy during the day; work at least 40 hours a week, write at night, early mornings, or on weekends.
- Don't cut scheduled publishing time for reasons you would not cut teaching time.
- Don't answer or check the phone/text and e-mail during publishing time unless it is publishing related or an emergency.
- Don't stop working on publishing if the urgent mater can wait until after your scheduled writing time. Ask yourself this question before you stop publication time.
- If you do stop working on scheduled publishing time, make it up the same week, such as at night or the weekend.
- Determine if working on publishing at home or school is more productive for you.
- If you write at home, try to deal with personal interruptions by asking household members not to disturb you when you are working. Having home office hours, an office with a door you can shut, and an office in an isolated area helps minimize interruptions that can wait until you are done working.

- If you are at school during your scheduled publication time, try to have your office in an isolated area, close your door, again don't answer or check the phone/text and e-mail, schedule the hours during quieter times, consider another location.
- Use assistance. Refer back to the list of 9 tips for assistance with teaching and 11 tips for publishing.
- Use general time management tips. Refer back to the list of 13 tips.

CHAPTER 6

MULTIPLYING PUBLICATIONS

CHAPTER OVERVIEW

As the chapter title suggests, the focus is on increasing the number of your publications.

- In the first section, I present the qualifications to look for in a coauthor, help you determine what you have to offer coauthors to get them to work with you, and give you ideas on who to get as coauthors and places to find them.
- The second section delves into the age-old problem of working with others in coauthor teams. I present ideas on how to plan, organize, lead, and control publishing teams.
- Section three discusses the benefits of specializing in a topic area. It also suggest taking your work to a regional, then national, and then journal to multiple your publications. You can also conduct longitudinal studies.
- The fourth section suggests using the total sample and running different levels of statistical analysis that can be sent to multiple sources of publications. Plus, it gives ideas on splitting the sample to allow for multiple analyses that can be sent to different publication sources.
- In the fifth section, I tell you how I took American samples and turned them into multinational studies.
- Section six suggested focusing on different variables in different papers or articles.

Publish Don't Perish: 100 Tips that Improve Your Ability to Get Published, pages 104–128
104

- The seventh section gets into the benefits of a scholarly reputation and provides tips on helping you to develop your reputation.
- The last section explains how editors republished my work to increase the total number of my publications.

CHAPTER OUTLINE

SELECTING AND GETTING COAUTHORS

One excellent way to increase your publishing productivity is to have coauthors to share the work. In my field, the vast majority of papers and articles are coauthored. Here I give you tips on selecting and getting coauthors with a focus on coauthor qualifications, determining what you have to offer, and who and where to get coauthors.

Coauthor Qualifications

Before I get into specifics of who to select and how to get coauthors, try to work with quality people, with the same niche that you have, as well as multidiscipline, who have strengths that you don't have.

Quality People
Always be open and seek to coauthor with others that have a good track record of publications. I know a guy who is very weak in research, but he managed to work with a few people who got him into two high level journals than I haven't been in. People with good publication records tend to be conscientious.

Conscientiousness
Seek out coauthors that do the work, at a quality level, and on time? If you are conscientious, it will be much easier to find and keep coauthors. I had a person ask to be a coauthor. I found out that he had problems working with other coauthors. He didn't want to do much work, the quality of his contribution was very low, and he got the work in late. What he really wanted to do was to put his name on other peoples work.

Same Niche
People with the same niche generally work well together. Just about all my coauthors have had the same niche as I do.

So I do recommend considering searching for coauthors with your niche.

Multidiscipline

I know, I just suggested working in your niche. However, if you work with people in other fields you can each use the data in different ways and get multiple publications together. Again, my niche is small business and entrepreneurship. However, I worked with a coauthor that is in finance. To tell you the truth, I really didn't understand all of his calculations, but I wrote and improved a good percentage of our papers and articles.

Different Strengths

My strength and interest is methods and statistics, so I tend to seek coauthors that will do the literature review and data collection. If you are weak at writing (English second language) seek coauthors that are strong, or as discussed in Chapter 1, get quality proofreaders. I am also good at writing research (not just English), and that was my strength in working with the finance guy.

What Do You Have to Offer Coauthors?

This is a short part of this section because I can't tell you what you have to offer. But I can tell you that when you approach someone to coauthor with you, you should be able to tell them how you can help them. One obvious thing potential coauthors want is more publications, so how can you help them? Will you be a quality, continuous coauthor? What qualifications do you have within your niche? Does your niche lend itself to multidiscipline coauthorship?

I suggested getting coauthors with different strengths than you. So your strength is commonly what you have to offer. Are you strong in theory and literature, methods and statistics, data collection, writing, or other things? Part of what you have to offer is discussed in the next section, working with coauthors.

For example, how much of the work, what parts, are you willing and qualified to do?

Who to Get and Where to Get Coauthors

Now that you know what to look for in coauthors and what you have to offer them, here are some ideas on who and where to get coauthors.

Mentors

As stated in Chapter 2, I have coauthored several papers and articles with my mentor Joel Corman. So following the ideas from Chapter 2, ask mentors to be coauthors.

Coworkers

A great place to find coauthors with your niche is at your school. Being in a small department at Springfield College, there is only one other faculty member who has a small business/entrepreneurship niche. I asked Robert Fiore to work with me and we have coauthored some papers and articles.

Conferences

I have more coauthors from conferences than mentors and coworkers. I met Matthew Sonfield at the Small Business Institute® (SBI) conference and we have done lots of research together; I'll give you more details later in this chapter. When I present a paper, I usually ask the people at the session if they would like to coauthor with me. I also go to other paper sessions and after the presentations ask if the person(s) would like to coauthor with me.

Journals

Contact authors you have referenced. When you read articles, consider contacting the authors and asking them if they would be interested in coauthoring with you.

People Who Contact You

I've had people contact me from around the world regarding my research. Rather than just answer questions, and hand out my questionnaire, I ask them if they would like to collect data in their country for me and we can coauthor papers and articles.

APPLICATION 6-1 (32)

What coauthor qualifications complement mine? What do I have to offer coauthors? Who should I approach to coauthor? How can I improve?

_____

_____

_____

_____

WORKING WITH COAUTHORS

Once you find coauthors, the publishing team has to be managed. So here are the four functions of management (planning, organizing, leading, and controlling) applied to coauthoring publications.

Planning

As you plan to work together, here are some things to agree on that will help everyone to be a quality, conscientious coauthor.

Objectives

What are the coauthors objectives, or what will you get out of the collaboration? Are you looking for the help of a mentor to get published, or in a higher level journal, or are you equal coauthors?

Topics and Number of Publications

Are you planning to do one publication or a series? Agreeing to multiple papers and/or articles help to multiply your publications. Once you work with people, the learning curve increases productivity. However, do dump nonproductive coauthors.

Target Publications

Where will you send your work—proceeding, journal, book? What specific conference, journal or book publisher? With multiples, you can have different targets. Again, know your school requirements. It is helpful to work with people with similar publication requirements, or those with higher levels that can help pull you up.

Time

What is the planned submission date? How long do you plan to take to do each step of the research process? How long of a turnaround time is expected for coauthors during the research process? Be cautious of people who don't want to commit to quick turnaround times because they may not be conscientious and can slow you down.

Author Sequence

It is helpful to agree on, and to be satisfied with, the author sequence. The sequence is commonly based on contribution. Contribution doesn't simply mean who does the most work. For example, when working with a mentor (Chapter 2), you may do most of the work, but if what you are doing is the mentor's ideas, the mentor may be making a greater contribution. As a mentor providing my expertise, I accept the last listing.

- *Being first author.* Some schools do consider the sequence of authorship. Many expect that you will be listed as first author on some of your publications. So don't take sequence too lightly or give it away too easily.
- *Equal contribution on publication.* The author sequence for equal coauthors is commonly alphabetical, but again

agree. Personally, I come to an agreement on a rank, and I often try to get multiple publications with the same co-authors to rotate the lead to avoid this problem.

- *Multiple publications.* If you plan to do multiple publications together, it is common to change sequence so others have a chance to be lead. This is my general approach; simple data collectors are always last.

Organizing

Organizing is about getting coauthors and distributing the work to increase your productivity. There is no one best way to share the work, but strengths of coauthors should be utilized. Here is my approach.

Distributing the Work

Work has to be distributed before and during the writing of the publication. To me, there are three key areas of research. There is a need for a good understanding of the literature, good methods and the statistics, and data collection (research proposal, which should be reviewed—Chapter 2) before writing the article. So the distributions of the work before and during the writing of the article are important decisions that should complement each other.

I always make it is "perfectly" clear, before we begin, what work I will do, and what each coauthor will do. This avoids confusion as the process unfolds. Who will submit the article and serve as contact author should also be distributed.

My Coauthor Roles and Responsibilities

My coauthor, Matt Sonfield, conducts and writes the literature review and discussion sections, with my input. I select the methods, run the statistics, and write the methods and results sections with his input. We have been getting people to collect data for us in other countries. We often suggest deleting, changing, or adding things to each other's sections highlighted in yellow so the other can easily see what has been added. We usually agree right away but may take a few draft rounds to come to an agreement.

I have also had two people from other countries collect data for me using my methodology. I wrote the papers and articles, with the input primarily in the introduction and discussion of the implications in their countries. Matt and I use this same input when we coauthor with other data collectors.

As a mentor, I generally give input to every stage of the research process without doing much, if any, writing. For writing, I give ideas to coauthors, but I try to let them do the writing. I do edit and proofread for them.

Leading

Here are some of the key areas of leadership.

Leader—First Author

The primary leadership role is usually assumed by the first author. But it can be any coauthor, but it often better to establish who the leader is. However, as in small teams, shared leadership tends to work well. The leader generally oversees the entire publishing process, including submitting the work and serving as the contact author. Contact authors often have the responsibility of notifying coauthors of acceptance decisions.

When I mentor, I generally take the lead through the complete work stage, even though mentorees are listed as first authors, but I let them submit and serve as contact author. With equals, we generally alternate being the leader on various publications. When I lead, I generally oversee, submit, and am contact author.

Relationships, Communications, and Trust. An important part of leadership is developing relationships so that coauthors work well together. Open and honest communications among all coauthors are critical to any team, even for only two people. Coauthors need to trust each other to do the work, at a quality level, and on time. Thus, the team and lead author deal with conscientiousness.

I'm willing to give people a shot at coauthoring with me, but if the relationship and communications don't work, or they are not conscientious, I try to get through the current publication. However, I decline any future proposed publications.

Decision Making

How decisions are made is up to the team, but participation is often the best approach. Getting back to planning topics, target publications, times, author sequence, and organizing the distribution of work, and who the leader will be on each publication are important decisions. Hopefully, everyone will agree and be satisfied with the decisions.

Maybe I'm lucky, or maybe I select quality, conscientious coauthors, but in my coauthored publications, we had shared decision making. At the time these decisions were made, everyone agreed. But things can change.

Conflict

Resolving conflicts is an important part of teamwork. As in any relationship, disagreement is inevitable. Coauthors can disagree at any and all stages of the publication process. For example, one may want a certain section of the article to read one way and someone else another way, or to include or not to include something in the article. Again, open and honest communications helps. All coauthors should give their input, and hopefully a consensus will emerge. If not, the leader should have the final say.

I've had disagreements during the publishing process. But knowing who the leader is, and that the leader will have the final say over disagreements, works well in my coauthor relationships. On occasion, I've lost and accept it knowing it is nothing personal. I also know that when I lead, I get the final say.

Controlling

The last function, controlling, is about making sure the work gets done and submitted. Controlling is clearly related to planning and organizing. The better the plan and organization, the easier it is for the leader the control the project.

Meeting Time Schedule

The leader is responsible for making sure all coauthors know and keep to the time schedule. How often coauthors need to be reminded to do their work and get it in to the leader is based on their level of conscientiousness. It is up to the leader to determine how much follow-up is needed for each coauthor. Some coauthors will give you a fast turn-around and not need any reminders. However, some may need several requests.

Un-conscientiousness

If coauthors are not getting their work in to the leader in a timely manner, action should be taken. I'm not going to try to tell you how to deal with people who are not conscientious, other than to stop working with them. But here is an example of how it was handled in a coauthorship I was involved in.

I once worked with a team of six coauthors. Two of us were very quick at getting in our work. The other guy was the leader. The two of us talked about it and agreed that we would give the other four coauthors a deadline to get their work in. If they didn't meet the deadline, they would be dropped as co-authors. A couple of them met the deadline one didn't do the work, and another believed that being at the ideas meeting was enough to keep him as a coauthor. So we dropped two co-authors. One accepted it for not sending in the work and the other one had hard feelings about it. The coauthorship of six ended. The leader and I continued alone to revise the work and get more publications.

APPLICATION 6-2 (3)

How will the planning, organizing, leading, and controlling be
managed in my coauthorships? How can I improve?

_____

_____

_____

_____

SPECIALIZING AND PROGRESSING

Specializing in one area and progressively improving your work
multiplies your work.

Specializing

In line with having a publishing niche (Chapter 3), specializing in a topic area is helpful. With specialization, you become
an expert in the literature of your topic. Thus, you can do multiple publications with the same literature foundation, or you
save lots of time by not having to do new literature reviews every time you research a new topic area.

Many schools also like to have faculty who are considered
experts in a topic, rather than generalist going in many directions. My area of specialization is business success vs. failure.
Through my literature search, I have more publications on this
topic than any other researcher. I've also been specializing in
family business research. More on this will be discussed in the
next two sections.

Three Stages of Progression

By taking the same research work through the three potential stages of publication, you can get three publications from

essentially improving the same work. In business, I can't state what is acceptable for other academic disciplines, AACSB accreditation accepts the practice of developing a paper for a regional conference that is published in its proceedings. Through the review process of getting written feedback on your paper, and through participant recommendations during the paper presentation, you can revise the regional conference paper and send it to a national conference. Following the same process, you can then send it to a journal.

Virtually everyone agrees that the paper to article can't be the exact same for the three different stages. The reason AACSB accepts the practice is to improve the work at each stage. The tricky part becomes in the amount of revisions needed to be considered acceptable to move through the three stages. I've never heard of any universally-accepted standards that all the different professional associations and journals agree with. So you may want to do your own research for the acceptable practice of taking a paper through to an article to multiple your publications.

Here is what I do. Now that I have over 300 publications, I am not as concerned about getting three for one every time. I tend to watch how many things I have in each stage of the publishing process (Chapter 1). If I'm in need of a journal article, I skip the conference route. But I still go through the three stages for most of my work.

Here are some tips on making sure your work is not the same at each stage of the publishing process. I pick a title for the regional conference and a different title for the national conference, but I tend to have the same title for national and the journal. Obviously, I make the recommended changes to improve the work at each stage. One thing that many conferences are doing to help you get through the stages without conflict is to publish a shorter version of your paper. Thus, you can chose to have some parts short, so that when you go to a journal, it is clearly different in that it is more complete.

Longitudinal Studies

Longitudinal studies collect and compare data over a period of time. So each time you collect data, you have another potential publication—or three if you go through the stages. I've actually only done one longitudinal study. Babson College was having its entrepreneurial research conference at the London School of Business. My mentor Joel Corman and I wanted to go to London to present, so we needed a research proposal because completed papers were not acceptable. So I came up with the idea of completing a longitudinal study.

We had done a study to determine factors that encourage entrepreneurial startups and existing firm expansion, so we re-surveyed the same sample and presented: Factors that Encourage Entrepreneurial Startup and Existing Firm Expansion: A Longitudinal Study Comparing Recession and Expansion Periods, which was published in the *Frontiers of Entrepreneurship Research.*

APPLICATION 6-3 (34)

Am I a specialist? Do I go through the three stages to improve my work and multiply my publications? Can I do longitudinal studies to multiple my publications? How can I improve?

LEVELS OF STATISTICAL ANALYSIS AND SPLITTING THE SAMPLE

In this and the next section, I focus on getting you to identify as many publishing angles as possible to multiply your publications. My basic tip here is to get as large a sample as you can so that you can break it into several subsamples that can be published. I believe that my procedures are ethical and accepted by the publication sources that accepted my work. Each paper or article clearly cites prior publications.

However, if you don't believe the procedures are ethical or accepted practice in your field, don't implement them in violation of your standards and publisher practices. Also, again you need to know your school publication requirements (Chapter 3). When you lower the level of statistical analysis and split the sample, you decrease your chances of getting accepted in higher-level proceedings and journals. If your school is only concerned about quality, it may not be worth your time and effort to change the level of statistical analysis and split your sample going for quantity.

My example in this section is based on my dissertation completed in 1993, and the topic was business success vs. failure. I wanted to better understand why some businesses succeed and others fail. My sample size was 108 successful and 108 failed matched pairs, for a total sample of 216, from multiple industries. By using the total sample with different levels of statistical analysis, splitting the sample, and extending my work, so far I have 29 publications—14 refereed journal articles (and one in-press) and 15 proceedings.

Levels of Statistical Analysis—Total Sample

I started with the total sample and used three levels of statistical analysis. First, let's get back to Chapter 4 for a moment to recall that we need to match the target publication. Different publication sources require different levels of statistical analysis. Thus, you can get multiple publications by targeting different sources.

Higher Level (Multivariate) Statistics

This was my primary publication with the objective of being accepted into a top level journal in my niche of small business. The level of statistics was logistic regression. My dependent variable was performance (success or failure) and I had a 15-independent-variable model to predict performance. The model was significant, and the article was published in 1995 (*Journal of Small Business Management, 33*[1]). Many top tier or higher level journals require multivariate level statistical analysis.

Lower Level (Bivariate) Statistics

For this research, I compared differences between the successful and failed businesses for each of the 15 independent variables using *t*-test and *chi*-square statistics. The paper was published in the Small Business Institute® (SBI) regional and national proceedings and the SBI sponsored *Journal of Small Business Strategy*. Many second-tier level journals are satisfied with bivariate level statistical analysis.

Descriptive Statistics

Here I asked open ended questions regarding reasons business fail and how to avoid failure, reasons businesses succeed, and advise for starting a business. This resulted in three articles and two proceedings. Using only descriptive statistics, giving only percentage of respondents stating their views, generally results in more of an informative article matching more practitioner oriented journals and magazines.

Informative Articles

Informative articles can also be based on higher levels of statistics without actually giving the details, like *p*-values. A good way to do this is to get your statistical articles published and then to use the analysis in a non-statistical approach giving how-to advice to practitioners who can't understand the statistical analyses anyway. You can also take research conducted by others and write an informative article based on the results.

Splitting the Sample

I split the sample by industry, compared single- to multi-industry, and split the sample by size. The problem with splitting the sample results in a smaller sample for the paper or article.

If the sample gets too small, it is difficult to get into a higher level journal. But if your school requirements include second tier journals and proceeding, splitting the sample can multiply your publications.

Industry

I broke the sample into five industries to develop a success vs. failure model for each industry. The five industries are: Services (one proceedings and article), Retailing (one article), Real Estate (one proceedings and article), and Construction and Manufacturing (one national and international proceeding). Note that the construction and manufacturing samples were rather small. This resulted in proceedings rather than journal articles.

Comparing Single to Multi-Industry Samples

Here I compared the total sample logistic regression model to each of the five industry models. There were differences in the total sample compared to the five industry samples. This results in one journal article, but I could have brought it to the regional and national conference level to multiply the publication.

Size

I broke the sample into businesses with 0–10 employees, resulting in one proceedings and one article. I planned to split the size in other ways, but I had so many publications going on that I never got around to it.

APPLICATION 6-4 (35)

Do I multiply my publications by conducting different level statistical analysis and splitting the sample? How can I improve?

EXTENDING YOUR WORK

This is a short section, but one that can really multiply your publications and it brings us back to the importance of coauthorship. One way to extend your work is to get coauthors. Coauthors can do a number of things to extend your work, such as take it to a different field of study and to collect data. I already gave an example of my work extending into finance. So I will now focus on data collection. As discussed with getting coauthors, you can contact authors in other countries and ask them to collect data for you and you can ask others that contact you to be a coauthor. In this section, I give an example of others contacting me, and in the next section, I give an example of contacting foreign authors to collect data for you.

I had Sanja Pfeifer from Croatia contact me for information about my success vs. failure research. So I asked her to collect data and coauthor with me. The primary work was to compare the success vs. failure prediction model in the USA vs. Croatia. This resulted in three proceedings and three journal articles. I wrote two of the articles and presented two of the papers in the USA as first author. Sanja wrote one of the articles with me as first author and presented a paper in Croatia as first author.

More recently, I had Claudia Halabi from Chile contact me about my success vs. failure research. She also collected data. The primary article compares the model in all three countries. So far we have published one journal article, have one in-press (I am first author), and one that we are revising to resubmit to another journal (she is first author). I have also presented three papers as first author in the USA.

APPLICATION 6-5 (36)

Do I get coauthors to extend my work? How can I improve?

_____

_____

_____

SPLITTING THE VARIABLES

Actually, changing the level of statistical analysis, splitting the sample, and extending your work, and as discussed in this section, splitting the variables can all be done together. However, here my example focuses more on splitting the variables. I will tell you that the niche is family business and that several coauthors and I have published 11 refereed journal articles and 47 proceedings so far over several years of work.

We began by conducting a literature review of important variables to family business and developed a questionnaire based on those variables. Below is a list of the 17 variables listed in the sequence the question was asked on the survey instrument:

1. Number of generations involved in the family business.
2. Percentage of managers that are and are not family members.
3. Percentage of family members that are men and women.
4. Input into decision-making by all family members in the business.
5. Conflict in the family firm.
6. Degree of success planning.
7. Use of outside advisors.
8. Time spent in strategic planning.
9. Use of sophisticated financial methods.
10. Influence of the original founder today.
11. Considering going public.
12. Top management style.
13. Debt vs. equity financing.
14. Years in business.
15. Number of employees.
16. Industry.
17. Form of ownership.

We first collected data in the USA. We went on to select various variables as the primary focus on a specific paper and/or article. For example, we compared the other variables by: generation, percentage of management, influence of the original founder, and years in business. Thus, the use of different variables as the dependent variable resulted in multiple publications. We haven't split the sample, but we have varied the level of statistical analysis.

Next we extended the family business work to have coauthors from other countries by contacting them and asking them to collect data for us. We are now up to having data from seven countries, with another in data collection, for a total sample size of more than 650 family businesses. With international data, we again select different dependent variables at the regional level focusing on each country separately. At the national level we tend to compare the various countries to the USA, and to each other. The studies with the better variables and test results are sent to journals.

APPLICATION 6-6 (37)

Do I get coauthors to extend my work? How can I improve?

_____

_____

_____

_____

REPUTATION AND PUBLISHING

Having a scholarly reputation can increase your ability to multiply your publications, and promoting your publications can help you to gain a reputation.

Reputation

You develop a reputation through publishing, especially in an area of specialization in your niche. The more publications you have in higher level proceedings and journals, generally the greater your reputation. But you can also enjoy a reputation being highly successful at lower level conferences as well. The greater your reputation, the more people want to coauthor with you, which again will multiply your publications.

When you send in an article to a journal, if the editor recognizes your name, based on your reputation, there is a chance that the editor will lean towards helping get your article published. The chances of this happening are even greater when you have published in top level journals and are sending to a lower level journal. Editors like to improve the quality of their journals, and having authors with national and international reputations helps.

With more than 340 publications and having people from all over America and from 56 other countries gives me a reputation that has multiplied my publications. Based on my research reputation, I have people ask me to mentor them as coauthors of papers and articles. Having multiple textbooks in the management field, an estimated million students globally have used my books, I recently had two publishers ask me to write textbooks for them. Many professors who don't use my management books, do know my name because of my reputation.

Promoting Your Publications

Unfortunately, it takes time and success to develop a reputation. However, through promoting your own work, you can help develop your reputation. Developing a reputation helps in publishing, but it also can lead to potential research funding and consulting jobs. Here are some ideas on promoting your publications:

Contact Authors

When you have an article published, go to your reference list. Contact the authors telling them that you have cited their work in your article, and enclose or attach at copy of your article. They could end up citing your article, which enhances your reputation. In getting coauthors, I suggested contacting authors to coauthor with you. By sending them a copy of your work, you present them with a sample of what you have to offer. Thus, increase your chances of working with quality coauthors.

Internet and Networking

Contact people to update them on your latest research topics and publications, and so on. You can network through e-mail, FaceBook and other social networking Web sites and other methods. Have your own Web site and include links to your publications. You should also be able to have a page on your school's website. But keep the website updated.

Join and online discussion forums, list servers, and so on. For example, The Academy of Management has AOM *Connect* connecting the Academy's global community. Its motto is Connect > Collaborate > Contribute with your colleagues. AOM members join the conversation at http://connect.aomonline. org. Your professional association may have its own networking connection.

Press Releases—Internal and External

The press can spread your name and enhance your reputation. Try to get your school to write them for you. But you can write press releases about your publications yourself as well. You may not have great success with the media, but don't forget that you have multiple types of press from your school, such as alumni magazines, school, and department newsletters.

When I get a publication, I send the information on campus to the Marketing and Communications Department (outside the college, alumni, and college wide publications), the dean and my department administrative assistant (school and department newsletter lists it). Thus, on campus I have the reputation as being the most prolific author.

Getting Your Article Read on the Web

To develop a reputation, people need to know your name, and they need to read your name and hopefully your abstract and entire article. One thing to realize is that most people find their articles by searching, not by browsing. To get your article to come to the top of a search, you need to have an effective title, keywords, and abstract with the keywords stated repeatedly throughout the article. I will provide tips on how to select a title and keywords, as well as how to write an abstract in Chapter 9, Empirical Research.

Contact Information

Always include your contact information (e-mail) in any press release and especially in your proceedings and articles. Doing so can help you get coauthors.

APPLICATION 6-7 (38)

What is my reputation, and can I enhance it? How can I improve?

HAVING YOUR WORK REPUBLISHED

You may have noticed, back in the Chapter 1 CV publication summary, that I have around 40 author-selected articles. Most of these are not articles that I sent to editors, but rather articles editors republished in their publication source. Here are examples.

Every year I present papers at the regional and national SBI® conferences. The editor of the *Small Business Advancement National Center Newsletter* (WWW.SBAERletter@sbaer.uca.edu) selects some of the best papers from SBI® and other conferences to include in the newsletter. Actually, the abstract is reproduced with a link to the entire article. SBAER has also taken some brief material from my *Entrepreneurial New Ventures* and *Small Business Management* textbooks (published through Cengage with coauthors Corman and Pennel). My work has been selected more than 10 times, which is a really nice multiplication of my publications without doing any extra work.

Five of my articles were selected by editors to be included in their collection of articles on family business—edited books. One of my success vs. failure articles was included in a multivariate statistics textbook as a good example of an article using logistic regression.

The *Harvard Deustro Business Review* (a joint publication by the Harvard Business School and the University of Deusto in Spain) translated one of my articles in Spanish and published it. I found out as one of my coauthors did a name search on the Internet and found it.

I also coauthored an article selected for publication and the editor had other scholars give a commentary on our work, following our article. As authors, we got to respond to the commentaries, chocking up another editor selected publication. Think about how many multiply publications I could have if I actually sent my work to such sources.

APPLICATION 6-3 (34)

Can I get republished? How can I improve?

_____

_____

_____

_____

SUMMARY OF TIPS

- Find quality coauthors.
- Tell potential coauthors what you have to offer.
- Ask your mentors and coworkers, and people that contact you, to be coauthors.
- Attend conferences and ask others to be coauthors.
- Read journal articles and reference lists and contact authors asking them to be coauthors.

- Help the coauthor team management the publishing process.
- Specialize in a topic area so you don't have to conduct new literature reviews.
- Develop your study and get three publications from it by publishing a regional and national conference paper, and then a journal article.
- Collect new data from your prior sample to compare differences over time—longitudinal studies.
- Take a sample and run different levels of statistical analysis and send the separate studies to multiple publication sources that match.
- Split your sample so that you have different studies that can be sent to multiple publication sources.
- Extend your work by having others collect additional data, such as data from other countries, to develop and publish new papers and articles.
- When you collect data, have multiple variables that can be used as the focus of a separate paper or article to provide multiple publications from the same data.
- Promote your work to help develop a reputation for your work by contacting authors, using the Internet and networking, and getting press coverage.

CHAPTER 7

REFEREED SOURCES

CHAPTER OVERVIEW

In this chapter, I expand on prior chapter coverage of publication sources that are refereed: proceedings, journals, and case studies.

- The first section focuses on whether or not you should write a paper based on the theme of the conference, and I give advice on how to use your presentation time to improve your work.
- The second section explains how to follow-up after submitting your article to a refereed journal, and how to deal with the revise and resubmit publishing decision.
- The last section gets into publishing case studies. It provides a list of resources that can help you write case, gives tips on getting published in textbooks and case sources, provides information on case professional associations, and provides tips for getting your cases published in refereed journals.

CHAPTER OUTLINE

   I. Proceedings and Presentations
      Theme or Not?
      Use Presentation Time to get Feedback
  II. Refereed Journals
      Following-up
      Revising and Resubmitting
 III. Case Studies
      Case Writing Resources
      Textbooks and Case Sources
      Case Professional Associations
      Case Journals and Journals with Cases

PROCEEDINGS AND PRESENTATIONS

As discussed in Chapter 2, there are several great advantages to attending conferences and presenting papers. An advantage to proceedings is the faster rate of publications of refereed papers. Many professional associations just provide a decision of accept or reject, no revise and resubmit. All accepted papers are published at the time of the conference meeting. Journal articles are usually much slower. Plus, as discussed in the last chapter, you can go to a regional then to a national conference to improve your work before submitting it to a journal, getting a three-for-one deal. Here are more tips related to helping you decide if you should write a paper related to the conference theme or not and how you can use your presentation time to your best advantage.

Theme or Not?

Conferences tend to have a theme. So if you have a paper related to the theme, it generally does increase your chances of acceptance, especially when the conference only accepts a limited number of papers. However, conferences usually take anything within the domain of their mission. They usually have tracks for the variety of papers they will accept. When deciding to write to the theme or not, consider the match between your niche and the theme and your goals.

Niche and Theme
Is the conference theme within your niche? If your niche and the theme match, you may not have too much extra work to do to write a theme paper. However, if they don't match, is it worth the time and effort to write a paper that is relatively new to you? The time and effort ties into your goals.

Goals
Do you only want a conference paper, or do you want a progression to a journal article? When making this decision, don't

forget the publishing requirements of your school, Chapter 3. If your school really doesn't count proceeding very highly, you may not want to spend time writing papers that you know will not go on to a journal. Remember that any time you are not working on a journal article, is not helping and can take away from, your goal of publishing journal articles. Focus on using conferences as a stepping stone to journal articles.

My Approach

I have written to the themes of the Organizational Behavior Teachers Conference (OBTC) to help increase my chances of acceptance, with success, knowing that I would only get a conference proceeding publication. My school does count proceedings. But one of the papers had a topic that was later turned into a top-level journal article that also resulted in good publicity for my *Management Fundamentals* (South-Western/Cengage), *Leadership* (South-Western/Cengage), and *Human Relations in Organizations* (Irwin/McGraw-Hill) textbooks.

I usually don't pay much attention to the theme at SBI® conferences because I know what it takes to get my papers accepted. I tend to write extra papers, without spending a lot of time, for the regional conference that I know are not at the level to be published in a journal. I do play the numbers game to increase my total publications. However, I also do get the three-for-one progression to a journal with the better papers.

Use Presentation Time to Get Feedback

Most of the presenters at conferences waste their time. Here is how you can better use your time. Although there are five sub-headings here, they are not sequential, they all go together.

Present Overview—Save Time for Feedback

One of the biggest mistakes presenters make is to find out how much time they have, say 20–30 minutes, and then they get their PowerPoint slide presentation to fit the exact time. In most cases people who come to your presentation will have a copy of the proceedings, so if they really want all the details, especially the literature review, they can read your paper. Save 10 minutes or more for the more important reason you are at the conference—to improve your work and progression from regional to national conference to a journal.

Listen—Don't Be Defensive

If presenters save time for a discussion and get negative feedback, they make the mistake of getting defensive and justify their work. Remember that you can't improve your work by talking and defining your work. You need to listen to others criticism for ideas on how to improve. So when someone criticizes your work, don't talk—listen. Also, when you get defensive, people with good ideas often don't give them because your behavior says I don't want your feedback.

Take Notes

Let's face it, no one really likes criticism. Our natural defensive emotions rise and it is hard to listen, rather than justify. Writing notes on how to improve your work can help keep you from talking, it can help keep you calmer, and it helps you remember the good ideas later when you can be more objective to the criticism you received.

Ask Questions

A good way to start the discussion, which you make sure you leave time for, is to ask a question like, how can I improve my work? If someone criticizes with a comment like, your methods are weak. Ask, what methods are better? If they say your statistics are too low level or wrong, ask what level is better or correct? If they say your lit review is missing important articles, ask what are the references?

You can also take this time to ask other questions, such as what journal is a good match where I could send this paper? How can I extend this into another paper/article? Is anyone interested in coauthoring an extension of my work? In addition to getting coauthors, I've had people get me in touch with others to collect data for me.

Get Proposal Reviews

Recall the suggestion to have your proposals reviewed, back in Chapter 2. The common approach is to talk to people outside of presentations. But I've actually presented dead-end papers in a few minutes and went on to present a proposal I have for another study. Audiences have been receptive to the switch and have given me ideas that I implemented to improve my methods. The balance of time between the current and proposed study can vary based on where you need the feedback most. You can simply ask a question or two related to your proposed study.

APPLICATION 7-1 (40)

Do I write for conference themes or not? Do I use my presentation time wisely? How can I improve?

_____

_____

_____

REFEREED JOURNALS

This section focuses on follow-up after you have submitted your article, with tips on following-up based on a rejection of your article and how to revise and resubmit to the same journal.

Following-up

Follow-up includes your contacting the editor if the decision is late, and following-up based on the publication decision—rejection.

Contact the Editor

Let's begin with the tip that if the journal says the review time is two months, and you don't hear within that time, contact the journal stating the date has past and ask for the review status. Often a reviewer has not sent in the review, so this reminder allows the journal to speed the process.

Acceptance Categories

The refereed review process generally results in one of three categories: reject, accept as is, or revise and resubmit. The not-very-common acceptance as is, clearly the best decision for you, has the only follow-up, generally, to review your article just prior to it being published. The revise and resubmit says you have a shot at it. I'll give you ideas on how to handle it in the next part of this section. So let's now discuss the rejection.

Rejection—Resend

The article can be rejected. In this case, your follow-up is to carefully read and make the recommended changes that will improve your work. This also means going back to Chapter 3 and selecting another journal that matches your work and then going back to Chapter 4 to match the new target journal. This is followed by submitting to another journal.

One other tip here is that if your article is rejected, you can contact the editor immediately thanking him or her for the ideas on improving your work and asking for a recommendation for another journal to send it to. Editors are often aware of other journals and may make recommendations. In fact, a couple of editor rejection letter I received actually listed a couple of other journals that might be interested in publishing my article.

Revising and Resubmitting

Because it is so rare to get an acceptance without any revisions, a revise and resubmit is generally great news because you have a foot in the door. I don't recall ever not getting an article published after revising and resubmitting. I usually get the acceptance after the first revision, but occasionally it takes a few rounds. Here are some tips that can help you get through the process.

The Revise and Resubmit Decision

The editor's letter typically asks if you want to revise and resubmit, with a date by which you should give a reply and it usually includes a resubmit deadline. So your first decision is if you will revise and resubmit, or decline the offer and send to another journal, as with a rejection.

If the criticism and work seem overwhelming at first read, take a day or two off and come back and re-read the letter before you say no to a revise and resubmit invitation. Time helps you deal with criticism (Chapter 1) and persevere. I almost always accept without delay, but here are a couple of examples of when I have declined.

Notice that I stated my success with revise and resubmitting. This is because I read the editor and reviewer comments and make sure I can reasonably make the revisions, if not I make changes and send to another journal. For example, I once was told that part of the revision was to collect new data. I did ask the editor not to have to collect more data, but the editor was firm, so I declined the revise and resubmit offer. I once had a situation in which so many major changes were required that I declined the offer. I made some of the changes and sent it to another journal.

Contacting the Editor With Your Decision and Asking for Clarification

I contact the editor quickly with my decision, usually stating that I will revise and resubmit before the deadline. I always give a revise and resubmit my highest priority and get it back in as soon as I can. However, if for some reason you can't meet the deadline, don't decline without asking for more time. Most editors will extend the deadline if you ask right away.

When the editor does a good job, you don't need any clarification. However, if the editor doesn't tell you what to do about ambiguity or contradiction in the reviewer comments, ask the editor for clarification. For example, if a reviewer states that you have used the wrong statistics without recommending an alternative, you can ask the editor. If one reviewer says the literature review is good but the other says it is missing some important studies, without listing them, ask the editor to clear up the contradiction.

Dealing with Criticism Objectively

The editor's role is to help you develop your work into a high-quality contribution integrating his or her ideas with those of the reviewers. Here are some ideas that might help you deal with criticism:

- *Helpful.* Remember that the editor and reviewers have put in time and effort to improve your article. They want to help you publish a great article.
- *Time off.* If the comments are painful, take a few days off. When you come back to make the revisions, you should be in a better state of mind to implement the rest of the tips below.
- *Let go—hear.* Let any negative feeling and resentment go so that you can actually understand what needs to be changed and why—hear and change as needed.
- *It's not personal.* Don't take criticism personally because it can't be personal as the reviewers don't know who you are, and you don't know who they are.
- *No defensiveness.* Don't be defensive and tell the editor and reviewers they are wrong or don't understand your work. If you are going to take this as your overall approach, I suggest not wasting your time. Just send your article to another journal.
- *Improve.* Focus on improving your work. Don't think of it as criticism but as ways to make your good article even better. If this doesn't work, here is one more idea.

- *Publication focus.* I remind myself that it's a game. What really matters is getting the acceptance so that the article is published. Why should I care if I make changes that I don't agree with? What difference does the change really make? I focus on doing what it takes to get another publication.
- *Aha.* Once you do "actually" become objective, you may realize that the editor and reviewers were right, or at least that they did improve your work. I recall during my dissertation that one of my advisors told me I had to run the regression for each industry. I resented doing so at the time, but recall (Chapter 6) that I ended up getting a separate journal article for each industry—aha! Thanks Dr. Robert Baeder.

Focus on the Editor's Comments

Always remember that the editor, not reviewers, makes the acceptance decision. The editor's letter should guide your revision. Therefore, do exactly as the editor tells you to do; in doing so, it is difficult for the editor not to accept your article. A good editor will clarify ambiguity and reviewer contradictions in the letter telling what needs to be changed to get an acceptance. If it is not clear, again, get clarification from the editor before making the revision.

Do What You Are Asked To Do, When Reasonable

I mean two things here. First, when you revise and resubmit your article, you have two options in dealing with recommended changes:

- *Change.* Make the change and explain how you changed as recommended.
- *Don't change.* Don't make the change and explain why you don't believe the change is an improvement.

My approach, as stated, is to make the change when it is relatively quick and easy. People don't like to be told that they are wrong, do you? When you elect not to make a change, the editor and/or reviewer may get defensive; thereby, increasing the chances of another round of revise and resubmit or a rejection. This especially holds true for editors because they have the final say. If you disagree with a reviewer, you can appeal to the editor, as discussed in the next subsection.

But recall that editors do select reviewers they believe are experts, so they do tend to listen to their recommendations. As a reviewer, I have held firm in some instances, refusing to give an acceptance until my change was made. In other instances, I have also told the editor my rationale for the change, but that it is OK with me to make the decision in favor of the author.

The second thing I mean about doing what you are asked means actually making the *real change*. When you make the decision to make the change, don't make minor changes when real changes are recommended and try to fool the editor and reviewer into thinking you made the change when you really didn't. That is, unless you want to increase the chances of a rejection or more rounds of revise and resubmits.

When You Don't Change

Keeping my focus on the editor, I generally do whatever the editor suggests. If I don't agree with the editor, I ask about not making the change before doing the revise and resubmit, such as the example of collecting new data. However, I don't make the changes suggested by only one reviewer when they require a lot of work. I always give a good thorough reason for not making the change, and I refer to the fact that the other one or two reviewers did not make this recommendation. I believe this helps give me leverage with the editor and reviewer making the suggestion to not push for the change.

But again, there is a risk of another round of revise and resubmit, so I don't do this very often. When you don't change, how you write your rationale for not making the change is important. Don't get the editor or reviewer defensive, so don't come out and say "you are wrong." State something like, "I/ we disagree with the recommended change because ...." "The change will not improve the article because ...."

Your Cover Letter

The cover letter is critical to getting the acceptance. It must clearly state how you have, or why you haven't, made each recommendation for change. The easier it is for the editor and reviewers to understand and find your changes in the article, the better the odds of getting an acceptance. However, you have to integrate the changes, not simply go through a checklist of items that don't pull together a revised article; thus, state how the changes fit together under the different recommendations. Also, when you focus on the editor's letter, you may not need to address some of the reviewer recommendations.

I find it easier to state how I made the changes, or not, as I revise the article. Therefore, I write the cover letter to the editor as I revise the article as a new document. I cut and paste the recommendations so that I can insert a statement for each comment about what I have done to make the change, or details of why I haven't made the change. I have one letter, in the same document, for the editor and one for each of the reviewers, unless the editor requires a response to only his or her recommendations.

Always be courteous; again don't directly say you are wrong. Be sure to thank the editor and reviewers for their suggestions that have improved the article. For example: "Doing …(suggested change) is a great idea and I have …(how you have changed it). By doing …. the article has improved."

Coauthors, Save, and Proofread

As suggested in coauthorship (Chapter 6), taking it to the next level, the decision to revise and resubmit or not should be a team decision, and who will make which changes and comment in the covering letter in the revision should be decided among coauthors. The same lead coauthor usually takes the leadership role through the revision. Another tip is to save the revision as a separate document so that you can refer back to the original paper, or revision drafts sent between coauthors. Again, never send or resubmit your work to an editor without a thorough proofreading (Chapter 2).

APPLICATION 7-2 (41)

Do I follow-up effectively? How do I handle the revise and resubmit? How can I improve?

_____

_____

_____

CASE STUDIES *(business)*

Cases can be either editor- or blind-referee selected, so I discuss both in this section. The cases that I'm writing about are cases focusing on contemporary real-world organizations that tend to address how and why questions for analysis. They are written for educational purposes, such as those in textbook and case sources sold individually, such as Harvard Business Cases. I also focus on case journals and journals that accept cases through a blind referee process. Writing cases based on secondary data only, commonly in textbooks, is relatively quick and easy. However, writing cases based on collecting your own primary data from real organizations published in refereed journals is relatively time consuming and complex.

AACSB accreditation views cases with teaching notes as equivalent to empirical research articles. But again, what are your school's publication requirements? A refereed case in a journal may be valuable at your school, whereas a case in a textbook or case source that are commonly author/editor selected may be of little value. So is it worth your time and effort to publish cases? If so, should they be refereed or not?

There are two forms of cases—teaching cases and research cases. In this section, I focus on teaching cases giving some basics starting with proving case-writing resources, then publishing cases in textbook and case sources, followed by providing some information on professional associations you can join, and end with some tips for writing cases primarily for journals.

I'd like to thank my friend and coauthor Herbert Sherman of Long Island University—Brooklyn Campus for reviewing this case studies section.

Case Writing Resources

If you want to develop a niche as a case writer based on primary data that are in refereed journals, I suggest referring to a book that is devoted to writing these cases. The recommended textbook for case writing is by William and Margaret Naumes (2006) *The Art and Craft of Case Writing (2nd ed.).* Both have served as editors of case journals (Bill—*The Case Research Journal;* Peggy—*The Case Journal*) and have been involved in case writing for innumerable years. Their book serves as an excellent "how-to" guide that takes the reader through every step of the case publishing process (research, writing, teaching note, and publishing outlets).

Also recommended is the case entitled "Case Research and Writing: Three Days in the Life of Professor Moore" by Armandi, Sherman, and Vega (*The Case Journal,* 1[1, Fall 2004], 4–30.) which provides a more concise version of the Naumes' text using a case format as the vehicle of instruction.

There are numerous websites that also have information pertaining to case writing:

- http://bingweb.binghamton.edu/~tchandy/Mgmt411/case_guide.html;
- http://www.schreyerinstitute.psu.edu/pdf/CaseWriting-Guide.pdf;
- http://tlt.its.psu.edu/suggestions/cases/write.html;
- http://www.casewriting.org/;
- http://med.fsu.edu/education/facultyDevelopment/case_writing_resources.asp)

There is also a listing of case professional association websites that provide case resource information stated shortly, but first let's discuss writing cases for textbooks and case sources.

Textbooks and Case Sources

In my field of management, just about every textbook has cases, including my *Human Relations in Organization, Management Fundamentals*, and *Leadership* (with Achua). In fact, after having paid Herbert Sherman for writing some of the cases for my textbooks, I wrote *Business, Society and Government Essentials: An Applied Ethics Approach* with Herb as my coauthor to write the ethical dilemmas within the chapters and three cases at the end of each chapter of the book. Herb can list each case in my textbooks as a publication, but our textbook only counts as one publication. Also, Herb's cases in my textbooks are not considered refereed. They are author/editor selected.

You can also publish cases in case sources, a list is below. Case books used to be common, but with custom publishing and easy access to online cases there aren't many case books being published anymore.

Suppliers and Publishers of Case Resources

Here is a list (changed to alphabetical order) taken from the North American Case Research Association (NACRA) web site. Go to (www.nacra.net) for links to their web sites for information on getting your cases accepted by case publishers:

- CasePlace.org
- CaseNet: South Western/Cengage
- Darden (UVa) Case Collection
- Electronic Hallway: Cases in Public, Non-Profit, & Health Administration
- European Case Clearing House
- Global View Interactive Cases
- HBS (Harvard) Case Collection
- IESE Publishing
- Ivey (Western Ontario) Case Collection
- Pearson Custom Publishing
- Primis Case Database: McGraw-Hill/Irwin Publishing
- School of Business & Economics, Wilfrid Laurier University, Canada

- XanEdu—Publisher of NACRA's Case Research Journal

Contact the Author

If you are interested in writing cases that appear in textbooks, you can contact authors of textbooks and ask if they are interested in having you write a case or cases for their textbook. I suggest starting with a textbook that you use now. Here is an example e-mail you could send to me or any author.

> Dear Dr. Lussier,
>
> I'm Joan Fisher, assistant professor of management at Salem State College in Massachusetts. I have been using your *Management Fundamentals* textbook for two years now. It is a great book; my students really like the variety and quality of your applications and skill development exercises. We particularly enjoy discussing your cases.
>
> I'm writing to offer to write a case for the next edition of your book, without any compensation. I'd like to get a publication, so I would expect that my name and college would be listed on the first page of the case stating that I am the author. Of course, the case and teaching note will be subject to your approval. I will give you permission to print the article and copyright to the publisher.
>
> [If you have any experience, even writing cases you use only in your own classes, list it in a new paragraph here, or don't list it.]
>
> Looking forward to hearing from you.
>
> Joan Fisher, PhD
>
> Contact info

Contact the Publisher

If you are interested in writing cases for any textbook or case publisher for both publication and compensation, contact the publishers. If you know any sales representatives for a publisher, you can talk to them about your interest. The sales representative should know who to contact within the company, usually the editor of the field you want to write cases in. You can also suggest specific text and case sources that you would be interested in writing cases for. Again, there is a list of suppliers and publishers of case resources you can contact, but they don't all publish cases and pay compensation for cases.

Case Professional Associations

If you are serious about writing cases as your niche, I strongly suggest joining a professional association for case studies for more detailed help and as an outlet for publishing your cases. Here is an example national professional associations and one of its regional associations for case writers followed by a list of affiliates and their journals.

NACRA

The North American Case Research Association (NACRA) is a collaborative organization of approximately 500 researchers, case writers and teachers, mostly in the business disciplines, who support each other's research and writing efforts (www.nacra.net). In addition to membership, professional case associations have conferences and publish case journals—*NACRA The Case Research Journal*. Affiliates also have conferences and have well-published case authors and even case journal editors (such as William and Margaret Naumes) conduct workshops on writing cases that you can attend. For example, there is also The CASE Association. CASE is the Eastern affiliate of NACRA and meets annually in May in conjunction with the Eastern Academy of Management (EAM).

NACRA Affiliates

Here is a list of NACRA-affiliated organizations taken from its web site, and I added their journals taken from their web sites to make it easier for you to find target journals for your cases. All have conferences. Go to (www.nacra.net) for links to their web sites:

- CASE Association (*The CASE Journal*)

- Society for Case Research & Annual Case Writer's Workshop (*Business Case Journal, Annual Advances in Business Cases, and Journal of Critical Incidents*)
- Western Casewriters Association (WCA, no journal listed)
- Southwest Case Research Association (*Journal of Applied Case Research*)
- World Association for Case Method Research & Application (*The International Journal of Case Research & Application*)
- ASAC (Administrative Sciences Association of Canada) Case Division (no journal listed, but gives access NACRA's journal)

Case Journals and Journals with Cases

One thing about case journals is that they typically use the same blind-review process as refereed journals. In fact, I refereed a case for a journal that also publishes cases even though when I agreed to be a reviewer, nothing was ever said about my reviewing cases. When I asked the *New England Journal of Entrepreneurship* editor (Herbert Sherman the founding editor of *The CASE Journal*) if I received the case in error, he responded no. "You write cases for your textbooks, so I know you can review cases." Two things you should do are to match the target journal and follow prior tips when writing cases. Many of these tips also apply to writing cases for textbooks and case publishers.

Matching
It is a good idea to select a journal to submit your case (Chapter 3) before you write the case study. You need to be sure to follow the author guidelines and match the cases in the journal (Chapter 4). The case journal may even give you a guide to actually writing a case study. Reading cases from the target journal is critical to ensuring a great match

Here are a few things to keep in mind and to match with the journal's cases:

- *Level.* There is a difference in a case written for under-graduate vs. graduate education and by different journals.
- *Length and detail.* Cases for graduates are usually longer and more details, and there are differences in journals.
- *Sophistication.* How complex is the case and its possible solution(s). Undergraduate cases are less sophisticated giving less problem areas to sift through to prioritize and solve.
- *Data.* Do the cases published have secondary only or primary data?
- *Methodology.* For primary data, what is your method of data collection about the organization: looking at its records, interviewing and/or surveying its people, observing its people and/or processes?
- *Access.* Can you get into an organization and collect data? Cases tend to focus on problems and don't tend to make an organization look good, so why should management let you in to conduct a case study? You will most likely need to convince them of the benefits of having an out-sider provide an objective view of the firm.
- *Teaching note.* One major difference between an article and a case is the need to write a teaching note to accompany the case that essentially gives teaching tips, provides possible answers to any case questions, and presents possible solutions to the case. So you also need to match the teaching notes from the journal.

Prior Tips

As with an article, follow the tips from the prior chapters, including writing a case proposal and having it reviewed, having the case pre-reviewed and proofread before submitting for publication (Chapter 2). Have coauthors and extend your work through a series of cases (Chapter 6). If you get rejected, be persistent and revise and resend to another publication (Chapter 1).

APPLICATION 7-1 (40)

Do I write case studies? Should I? How can I improve?

SUMMARY OF TIPS

- Writing a paper for the conference theme increases the chances of acceptance.
- Have goals for your research. Do you want just a proceedings or to go through the regional, to national, to journal process.
- Save presentation time to get feedback on how to improve your work to take it to the next level of progression.
- When getting feedback, don't be defensive—listen and take notes, and ask questions.
- After a presentation, get a review of a proposal for an extended or different paper.
- If you don't hear from the journal editor within the stated review and decision time, contact the editor and ask for the status of your article.
- When your article is rejected from one journal, revise based on the reviews and resubmit to another journal.
- When making the revise and resubmit decision, determine if you can "reasonably" make the required changes. If not, sent the article to another journal.
- If two reviewers contradict each other and the editor has not made the required revisions clear, contact the editor for clarification before making the revisions.
- Deal with criticism objectively by taking some time off, letting resentment go, not being defensive, not taking it personal; focus on the comments being helpful to improve your article that will be published.

- When making revisions, be sure to concentrate on the editors comments.
- Make the recommended revisions that are reasonable.
- If you don't make a revision, explain the rationale without getting the editor or reviewer defensive.
- The cover letter to the editor should clearly state how you have revised, or why you haven't changed, to address the editor's and each reviewer's comments.
- Have coauthors share the revising, save copies as you revise, and proofread before resubmitting.
- Know your schools publishing requirements. Case studies published in refereed journals may have high value at your school, but non-refereed cases may not.
- There are resources (see the list) to help you write cases.
- If you are interested in publishing cases in textbooks and case sources, contact the authors and publishers.
- Case writers should join a professional association (such as NACRA and its affiliates) for assistance in writing cases and as an outlet for publishing cases.
- Before writing a case, select a publication source and be sure to match the other cases while writing the case, and follow prior tips.

CHAPTER 8

NON-REFEREED SOURCES

CHAPTER OVERVIEW

So far, the focus has been primarily on publishing refereed conference papers and journal articles, with a discussion of cases in the last chapter. In this chapter, I expand publishing to non-refereed sources.

- In the first section, I discuss publishing informative articles in editor-selected journals. Tips are given on selecting topics for practitioners, and I explain how to write for practitioners.
- The second section focuses on editing books. I discuss how you can edit conference proceedings, a book for profit, a book for academic recognition, and provide some tips on coordinating the book as its editor.
- In the third section, I explain what book reviews are, suggest contacting the book review editor to get an acceptance of your review before writing it, and discuss the five parts to include when you write a book review.
- The forth section describes how writing a textbook is an entrepreneurial venture, your need to have a competitive advantage to succeed, that to get a contract to write a book you generally need to write a prospectus (I explain the parts of it) and 2–3 sample chapters, and how to get a publisher.
- In the last section, I discuss writing textbook supplements for editor selected publication and compensation and reviewing textbook reviews for non-publication compensation.

Publish Don't Perish: 100 Tips that Improve Your Ability to Get Published, pages 152–176
Copyright © 2010 by Information Age Publishing

CHAPTER OUTLINE

I. Editor Selected Journals
   Informative Articles
   Selecting Practitioner Topics
   Writing for Practitioners
II. Editing Books
   Proceedings
   Edited Books
   Edited Textbook Supplements
   Academic Edited Books
   Coordinating the Book
III. Book Reviews
   Overview of Book Reviews
   Contact the Book Review Editor
   Parts of the Book Review
IV. Textbooks
   Entrepreneurship
   Competitive Advantage
   Prospectus and Sample Chapters
   Getting a Publisher
V. Textbook Supplements and Reviews

EDITOR SELECTED JOURNALS

Recall (Chapters 1 and 3) that editor-selected articles are not blind peer reviewed or that they are not blind reviews, and that the magazines and journals are more commonly targeted to practitioners. Therefore, the editors are seeking primarily informative articles and the writing style is different than academic. Thus, in this section I explain differences between informative articles and the writing style compared to conceptual and empirical refereed journal articles.

Also, recall that editor-selected articles are less prestigious than refereed journal articles. I must emphasize that you consider the publishing requirements of your school. If editor-selected articles in practitioner oriented journals don't count, or not worth much, maybe you should not publish them. However, if they are of value, go for it. Also, recall (Chapter 6) that you can publish an academic conceptual and empirical article and then also write a practitioner article to multiple your publications.

Informative Articles

I'll begin by explaining the difference between types of informative journals and the difference between informative and academic journal articles.

Practitioner vs. Trade Journals

Informative articles are commonly published in both practitioner and trade journals. *Practitioner journals* are aimed at a particular professional market. They can be of high quality, such as the *Harvard Business Review.*

Trade journals are generally published for its membership in the professional or trade association, and they are generally less selective about the quality of the content. For example, the *Clinical Leadership & Management Review* (*CL&MR*) published by the Clinical Laboratory Management Association. Thus, generally, practitioner journals are more prestigious, but your school may not classify the difference between the two.

Changing Reviews to Blind

Practitioner and trade journals can also be peer reviewed, such as the *Academy of Management Perspective*, but this changes the status to refereed articles. *CL&MR* is not known to be a refereed journal because the peer review is commonly author known to the practitioners who review the articles. However, I asked the editor to blind review my articles, which was done so that I could change the classification of my articles to refereed journal articles. You may want to ask; all the editor can do is say no.

Informative vs. Academic Journal Articles

Here are some major differences; I use practitioners to refer to both practitioner and trade articles because they are both targeted to non-academics:

- *Practitioners.* Informative articles target readers/subscribers are practitioners, vs. academics.
- *Literature.* Practitioners don't want to read lengthy literature reviews, academics do.
- *Methods.* Practitioners don't want to read lengthy research methodology, academics do.
- *Statistics.* Practitioners, generally, can't understand or don't want to read beyond descriptive statistics, academics want advanced statistical analysis.
- *Implications.* Practitioners want to know in clear English how to implement your recommendations to them. Academics say they want implications to practitioners, but it is just as important, and often more so, to have implications to extend theory and further research. Academics generally don't want to read detailed "how to" advice for practitioners.

Selecting Practitioner Topics

If you have an idea for a topic, or want to get a topic, contact the target journal editor to discuss topics. You can also take one of your empirical studies and write a practitioner article based on your work. You can also write a case study for practitioners.

Contact Editors

I don't usually contact editors of academic journals, but I always do with practitioner journals. If you have a topic, but are not sure if it is a good one for your target practitioner journal, contact the editor and discuss if the topic is of interest to the readers of the magazine or journal. If the editor is not interested in your topic, or you don't have a topic idea, ask or e-mail the editor for a topic. If you get the editor to say the topic is a good one, there is a very good chance of getting your article accepted. A good part of the reason is practitioner journals do edit your work. My coauthor Matthew Sonfield, who is a very good writer, had an article accepted in the *Harvard Business Review*, and he was surprised to see how substantially his article had been changed.

Academic to Practitioner Article

You should understand the differences between an academic (conceptual and empirical) article and an informative practitioner article. So after reading the author guidelines and articles in your target magazine or journal, you should understand both the content and the writing style that you need to match. Thus, in most cases, don't try to take your academic article and make some minor changes. Write a new informative article that really matches the target publication.

Case Studies

A case study can be written for practitioners. However, the practitioner case study is different from the writing of a case study presented in the last chapter, Case Studies section. For practitioners, you are focusing on presenting how one or a few organizations use a business practice or solve a problem with the focus on giving advice to practitioners on how they can implement the practice or solve the same problem in their organization. So, if you are writing a case study for a practitioner journal, be sure to read case study articles in the target publication to understand the content and writing style.

Writing for Practitioners

Based on the above differences between an informative and academic article, you should understand that the contents of your practitioner article and your writing style has to be different to properly match your target publication. Thus, you need to follow the tips for matching publication sources from Chapter 4 for all types of articles. Here are a few tips that generally, but again check your match, apply to practitioner articles.

Length

If you have read some target practitioner articles, you most likely realize that the length of the articles are much shorter than academic articles. They often have word or page limits stated in the author guidelines.

Writing Style

Here are some general ideas to follow when writing for practitioners:

- *Concise.* Keep it short; get to the point. Paragraphs and sentences are shorter.
- *Vocabulary.* Avoid academic and other jargon practitioners may not understand. Your vocabulary should be clear and easy to read and understand. Clearly define any academic terms using vocabulary that practitioners can relate to.
- *Examples.* Use lots of examples to give practitioners ideas on "how to" implement your recommendations.
- *Heading and bullets.* Use lots of them, as I have done in this book, to make it easier to skip over, skim through, and read and follow your recommendations.

Title and Introduction—Implications to Practitioners
The title and introduction are usually short and states implications, as it tries to catch the readers' attention. It can also ask questions to get the readers' attention. Here is an example title and introduction from Robert N. Lussier, *Clinical Leadership & Management Review, 19*(6, 2005), E4, 1–4.

MAINTAINING CIVILITY IN THE LABORATORY

> Has your staff been disrespectful or outright rude to you? Have they been rude to each other? If so, that's an example of incivility. Incivility leads to decreased work effort, productivity, and performance. When incivility is not curtailed, job satisfaction and professional loyalty diminish. Although incivility is on the rise in the workplace, few laboratory managers have been trained to deal with this problem. As a result, they accept or ignore acts of incivility. This article offers guidelines on ways to maintain civility in your laboratory.

Recommendations
Practitioners tend to read your article to learn ways to increase performance. Different headings may be used, but the reader wants to know what advice you have for them.

Continuing my same *CL&MR* article, here is an example. Note that the introduction above was followed by heading/sections on Incivility—A Problem in the Workplace, Causes of Incivility, and Consequences of Incivility. Also, I am only including the titles of the seven recommendations; detailed advice under head heading is not provided here.

Maintaining Civility

There are a number of methods that managers may use to contain, correct, and curtail incivility in their laboratory:

1. Set zero-tolerance expectations.
2. Lead by example.
3. Do not hire uncivil employees.
4. Teach civility.
5. Watch and listen for incivility—encourage whistle-blowing.

6. Take corrective action when incivility occurs—no exceptions.
7. Conduct post-exit interviews.

This civility article was not based on any prior work in this area. I wanted to get a quick article, so I called the *CL&MR* editor and asked for topics she was interested in publishing. From a list of a few topics, I picked civility and did a literature review (the articles do have footnotes). Based on the review, in about 8 hours I wrote the article and submitted it, and it was published in the next issue. So it took less than a couple of months to go from calling the editor to publishing and article. Also, as suggested, I asked the editor to do a blind review, so the article was a refereed journal article for practitioners.

APPLICATION 8-1 (43)

Do I write practitioner articles? Should I? How can I improve?

_____

_____

_____

_____

EDITING BOOKS

As an editor of a non-refereed book, you get other authors to contribute their work to your book. Thus, the term multi-authored work is also used to refer to edited books. Getting a publication as the editor of a book may be harder than it sounds. It may not be easy to get a publisher and authors to contribute. The contents must have a logical structure to attract a publisher and authors. There are different types of edited books (proceedings, textbooks, supplements, and academic) that I discuss here, and I also briefly discuss coordinating the edited book.

Once again I must emphasize that you consider the publishing requirements of your school. If editing a book and contributing to an edited book are not worth much, maybe you should put your publishing time into other sources. However, if they are of value, go for it. Editing some types of books can also be profitable. I've been the proceedings editor of the SBI Eastern Conference several times (to be of service, not really for the publication), but I never edited a book.

Proceedings

Being the editor of a conference proceeding is usually a matter of being an active member of the professional association and being appointed or volunteering to be the editor. The easy part is that you don't have to get authors, as they send in papers. The harder part is putting the accepted papers into a logical structure and not making any errors, such as not including someone's paper; I've had this done to me, and I've done it to others. Having good quality assistance (Chapter 5) that can do the work for you is a great help.

Selection of papers included in the proceedings is commonly blind refereed. It is common for the editor to get a refereed paper in the proceedings and also to get a non-refereed publication as editor of the proceedings. It is common to write a letter from the editor, list and thank the reviewers, and of course provide a table of contents.

Edited Books

An edited book can be a one-time book or a series. Edited books are often textbooks or supplements to textbooks. But there are other types of books, such as for practitioners. You can edit a book or supplement, or contribute to one. I've never edited a book or written a chapter in a book, but I do have some colleagues that have. Editing a book requires getting other authors to contribute their work.

Compensation

My focus is on editing books to make a profit for the publisher and to get compensated for time and effort. With a book, authors may expect to get paid to write a chapter, so as editor or author you need to be prepared to negotiate compensation. The editor the publisher should be able to help you through the process. As editor, after discussing common payouts with your publisher, be sure to follow the negotiation rule below to help ensure that you do in fact get a reasonable compensation for yourself.

Let the Other Person Make the First Offer

For this example, let's assume the publisher says the average paid for writing a chapter is $1,000. When getting authors, don't come out and say I will pay you $1,000 to write a chapter. Ask the person, how much do you expect to be paid for writing a chapter in my book? If the author says $500, agree to the compensation. If they say $2,000 try to negotiate down to the average.

Edited Textbook Supplements

In my field of management, I don't know of any edited textbooks, but here is an example of an edited supplement. I met a guy at a conference who did annual literature reviews in management, selected the best articles related to the course he was teaching, and had the students read the articles.

He got the idea of getting a publisher to make his selected management articles into the *Annual Edition of Management*. The edited book was sold as a supplement to management courses. The editor not only selected the articles to be included, he made an Instructor's Manual listing popular textbooks stating which articles could be used with each chapter. In addition to selecting the articles, the editor had to get permission to republish the articles in his book, which often required a fee. His royalties minus republishing fees resulted in a profit for the publisher and editor. The editor got an annual non-refereed edited book publication and the authors got a republication of an editor selected article.

Academic Edited Books

There are also edited books for academics. Although they can provide compensation to the editor, they are usually are not a lucrative as textbooks and supplements. I've been republished in two family business-edited books. Because the articles were already written, I gave permission to republish my articles without any compensation. I believe the editor was looking for a publication and didn't make much money.

There are also edited series or annual edited books, such as *Advances in Strategic Management*. These annuals tend to focus on hot topics and the trends in the field. Academics may not even get compensation for editing. Academic editing is commonly done to contribute service to the profession. To edit an academic annual, you usually have to develop a reputation in your niche.

Being an active member of your professional association develops your reputation and it also helps you make connections to become an editor. These connections also help you to be an editor of a special issue of a journal. As editor, you get a non-refereed publication, but contributing authors can be selected through a blind referee process. Therefore, you can get a refereed article in an academic edited book.

Coordinating the Book

The editor needs to determine the sequence of the authors work into parts and chapters. A challenging task of editing a book is getting the multiple authors to write in a similar style so that there is some consistency throughout the book. This is especially important for textbooks. So you need to carefully develop a format that everyone agrees to follow. The editor also needs to get everyone to get their work in, and on time. In coordinating your work, I suggest following the suggestions about working with coauthors in Chapter 6 to plan, organize, lead, and control the edited book process.

APPLICATION 8-2 (44)

Have I edited a book? Should I? How can I improve?

_____

_____

_____

BOOK REVIEWS

In this section, I begin with an overview of book reviews, followed by recommending contacting the book review editor before writing a book review, and end with a list of the five parts to a book review.

Overview of Book Reviews

Some journals include book reviews. Books that are reviewed by academics are usually academic books, rather than textbooks. Reviewing a book is a fairly quick and easy non-refereed publication, but doing so is not very high on school publication requirements. I've only written one book review. If you already read the book, all you have to do is write the review.

Basics

Here are some book review basics:

- *Objective.* The primary reason you write a book review is to let the reader know what the book is all about and whether or not it is worth buying. It's not about you.

- *Balanced.* Both the strengths and weaknesses of the book should be discussed. Don't be overly critical and abusive of the book.
- *Informative and interesting.* The entire book review should be informative and interesting right from the start through the end.

Get Your Book Reviewed

A good book review can increase sales. So if you have written a book, get a friend to write a book review in a journal for the publicity. I had a man I just met ask me to go to Amazon.com and write a positive review for his book.

I write textbooks, which are not commonly reviewed. However, unknown to me until a friend told me about the article, John Bigelow published "Managerial Skills Texts: How Do They Stack UP?" In the *Journal of Management Education, 17*(3, 1993), 399–415. The article compared nine books including my *Human Relations in Organizations: Applications and Skill Building* (McGraw-Hill/Irwin, 1990). In the conclusion Bigelow wrote, "If I were teaching a general Organizational Behavior-type course, I think I'd go with the Lussier text..." I believe this helped increase the sales of my book. As I wrote this book in 2010, my HR textbook was in its 8th edition.

I've never asked anyone to review my books, but if you would like to do a positive review of this book, *Publish Don't Perish,* for a journal I'd appreciate it. It might be a book that book review editors would like to have. But as suggested next, ask.

Contact the Book Review Editor

If you are interested in writing a book review for a journal, contact the book review editor with one of two approaches:

- *Read book.* Ask the editors if they are interested in a review of a specific book you already read, or simply
- *Seeking book.* Ask the editor if there are any books the journal would like to have you review.

Various journals do have different requirements for book reviews. The book review editor may provide a book review guide. There is usually a recommended length. But as usual, read other reviews in the journal so that you can match the reviews of the journal.

Parts of the Book Review

Although there are differences, there are commonly five parts to the book review. However, the sequence of the last four parts can vary.

Reference
Be sure to include: The authors' or editors' names and initials, title of the book, edition (if given), date of publication, publisher and city/state, ISBN number, hard or soft cover, number of pages, price.

Introduction
The introduction gives an overview of the book and how it fits in the topic field of study. State who the target readers of the book are. What is the objective, usefulness of the book, or why should anyone read it? You should be able to get this information in the preface and through the book.

Contents
Based on length of the review, contents are listed by sections and chapter and often topics within the chapters. This is where book reviewers often place too much emphasis. Readers of your review want to know what the book is about, but don't get into too much detail. If you provide a well-written review, readers will decide if they want to buy the book and get all the contents. This is the easiest part of the review because it comes straight from the book.

Highlights
What is the primary message or value of the book? You can't give details of everything, so what are the most impor-

tant contributions of the book? Here the essence of the book is discussed succinctly. Critique the author's premises and arguments. This section can be relatively easy when the author keeps to a main focus throughout the book, but when there are multiple seemingly unrelated topics, it can take time and thought to select the highlights. A good critique always takes time to develop.

Evaluation

What was done well (strengths)? What was not done very well (weakness or limitations)? Remember to give a balanced evaluation. This section takes the most judgment on your part and is what the reader wants to know. Does the book meet its basic objectives to meet the needs of the reader? A purchase recommendation may be included. If you don't like the book, again don't be overly critical of the book and unkind and abusive in your criticism.

APPLICATION 8-3 (45)

Have I written a book review? Should I How can I improve?

_____

_____

_____

TEXTBOOKS

As stated back in Chapter 4, textbooks take a lot of time to write and are often not given much weight for tenure and promotion. Again, know your school's publication requirements. Ask your department chair and dean if they recommend writing a textbook. But remember, like athletes and professional athletes, there are thousands of professors but relatively few textbook writers. The odds of getting published in other sources are much greater.

Entrepreneurship

As a textbook writing, you should realize that you are an entrepreneur because you are taking a large risk and you don't get a pay check. You are not an employee of the publisher, you get a royalty (commonly 10–15% of the price of the textbook to the bookstore) based on sales. It took me more than 1,700 hours to write my first textbook, then it went into production and nine months later it was published. Next I had to wait for six months of sales before getting a royalty check. So it was somewhere between 2 ½ to 3 years before I got a check. Plus, I didn't make extra money as I let my consulting business slide and didn't teach extra courses during the year or summers. If my school was the only one using the textbook, I would have only made pennies on an hourly base.

To really pay, the textbook needs to sell well and go into multiple editions. My first book, *Supervision*, went into second edition and when companies merged, it was dropped. But my other textbooks are still going into new editions, although I have had to change publishers for two of them. Thus, the extra money I earn though textbook writing has increased my standard of living substantially.

Steve Robbins wasn't having great success with proceedings and journals, so he decided to focus on management textbooks. As a best-selling author, San Diego State University was pleased with the publicity he brought to the school. Robbins was so successful that he retired from teaching at age 50 to focus on textbooks and in his early 60s he essentially let coauthors do the revisions. He retired very rich, and the University lets him continue to list San Diego State without any indication that he hasn't taught there in more than a decade.

However, can you be another Steve Robbins? I recommend having an established publication record of proceedings and refereed journal articles and tenure before considering writing a textbook. I also recommend that you keep presenting papers and writing articles while writing the textbook(s), as most textbook authors do, including me.

Competitive Advantage

Getting a textbook publisher is not about how well you can write; it's about presenting the material in a superior way (competitive advantage) so that you get professors to require your textbook rather than competitors for their courses. Keep in mind that professors, not students, make the textbook decisions. Although textbooks are not considered refereed publications, your prospectus and textbook will be reviewed by your peers, not students.

If you want to publish a textbook in an established field that already has textbooks, you have to come up with a competitive advantage. You need to clearly state how your book will be better than the competitors. It has to answer these overlapping questions:

- What will my textbook do better than others?
- Why would anyone new adopt my textbook over the competitors?
- Why would someone already teaching the course change to my textbook?

My Competitive Advantage

My primary competitive advantage, which is clearly stated in the preface of each of my textbooks is as follows. I have the most "how-to" manage textbooks. Students not only learn the concepts, they apply the concepts and develop skills they can use in their personal and professional lives. My textbooks offer more variety and higher quality applications and skill development exercises than the competitors.

Your Reputation

Having a name in your field for conference and journals and/or textbooks is part of your competitive advantage. If publishers know your reputation, they are more apt to publish your textbook. Before I developed a reputation, I had many editors reject my textbooks. I've had editors contact me recently asking me to write a textbook for them. Also, if professors

know of your reputation, they are more likely t
that your book be published and they are more
your book. Part of your reputation is also where
school and where you teach.

Different But Not too Different

You want it to be different from the competition, but not
too different or major publishers will not want to publish your
book and not many professors will adopt it for their classes. For
example, for more than 35 years the structure of the principles
of management textbook has been on the four functions of
management. Over the years a few books have come out with
different structures, but they haven't caught on and are not revised. Steve Robbins stated that most of the changes take place
in the margins, such as new boxes with examples, applications,
and skills material.

Prospectus and Sample Chapters

If you want to write a textbook, you need to write a prospectus. Publishers provide guidelines for writing a prospectus that
you should follow, but here are the common parts. Note that
the prospectus is one document and each of the sample chapters are separate documents.

- *Market.* What course(s) can use the textbook?
- *Competitive advantage.* List competitive textbooks and state
  your competitive advantage over them. See above discussion.
- *Comparisons.* Compare your book to specific competitors
  stating how you are better. List specific chapters and page
  numbers to compare to your stated advantages in your
  prospectus.
- *Supplements.* State if you plan to have an Instructor's Manual, test bank, PowerPoint slides, videos, Web site, etc.
- *Credentials.* What are your qualifications to write this
  book—how many years have you taught the course? State

publication in the topic and general field. I write a few paragraphs and attach my full CV.

- *Status.* How much work have you already done, and when can you have the final manuscript completed?
- *Contents.* Have a content in brief listing all sections and chapters on one page, followed by the contents including level 1 and 2 headings for each chapter. Most publishers and potential adopters will want you to have essentially the same contents as the competitors, so be sure to develop your contents based on the competition.
- *Sample chapters.* Editors usually want 2–3 chapters to judge your ability to include content and writing ability.

Have your prospectus and sample chapters pre-reviewed for improvements. If the editor likes your work, it will most likely go out for peer review. Therefore, the prospectus and sample chapters need to be well written. Remember that reviewers are looking for reasons to reject your work. You want reviewers focusing on the content; you don't want them pointing out errors. So be sure to do a good job of proofreading (Chapter 2).

Getting a Publisher

If you are teaching the course, you should be aware of the various publishers in your field. If you are not sure, check with your reference librarian for a list of publishers. Here are a few things to consider when selecting a publisher. Do realize that I am talking in generalities; there are exceptions to what I'm stating here concerning large vs. small publishers.

Larger Publishers

The larger textbook publishers (i.e., Cengage, McGraw-Hill, Pearson) generally want:

- *Sales Volume.* They want textbooks for the main large markets, such as principles courses with large enrollments.

My *Human Relations, Management Fundamentals,* and *Leadership* textbooks are with large publishers.

- *Titles.* They also want multiple textbooks for the same course that are slightly different, but not too different so they can offer new books each year.
- *Authors.* They tend to have authors with good reputations.
- *Royalty.* From my experience, they pay 15%.
- *Support.* They tend to pay others to do supplements to the textbook and provide a Web site for you book.
- *Marketing.* They tend to have sales reps and do a good job of promoting your book in the first year.

Smaller Publishers

The smaller textbook publishers (i.e., Information Age, Sage, Human Kinetics, Waveland, Routledge) generally want:

- *Sales Volume.* They are more willing to publish textbooks for large and niche markets that have lower sales. My *Sport Management* book was dropped by South-Western/Cengage and gladly accepted by Human Kinetics that specializes in this area. The big publishers rejected my *Business, Society and Government* textbook, but Waveland accepted it; and I went directly to Waveland for my *Research Methods and Statistics for Business* book and to Information Age Publishing (IAP) for this book.
- *Titles.* They recruit to have a book in their areas of publishing, and tend to be willing to publish books that are really different.
- *Authors.* They are more willing to publish authors without reputations.
- *Royalty.* From my experience, they pay 10% but may increase the rate up to 15% with sales greater than a target number, say 10% on the first 2,000, 12% on 2,001–4,000, and so on up.
- *Support.* The smaller are less likely to pay others to do supplements to the textbook and may not provide a Web site for you book.

- *Marketing.* They don't tend to have sales reps, keeping cost down, but they can do a good job of targeting your book through mail/e-mail brochures.

The books I have with the larger companies are my most profitable, but I am happy to be with the smaller publishers as well. So like with refereed journals, I would generally start with the better known name larger publishers, although as stated I did go directly to smaller publishers.

Contacting Publishers

After selecting a publisher, you can talk to a sales rep if you have one, or go directly to the editor stating your interest. You can look in the first few pages opening credits of a textbook in your field to find the editor's name, or just contact the company and ask who the editor is in your field. If the editor is interested in publishing your textbook, the next step is usually to send your prospectus and sample chapters.

When I e-mailed the IAP editor introducing myself and telling him I wanted to write this book, I asked him to call me. But he e-mailed back saying great idea, spend me a prospectus, no sample chapters needed. After he offered me a contract to write the book, we spoke on the phone.

No Guarantees

When an editor is willing to read your prospectus and even if it makes it to review, doesn't mean you have a contract. I had one book an editor wanted to publish and it got good reviews, but the publishing committee turned it down. Although very rare, I even had a contract and wrote the book, only to have a new editor take over the project and decide not to publish the book; threatening to take legal action, I did get some compensation and had the textbook published with a different company. So there are no guarantees. You haven't really succeeded until you get free copies of your published textbook and a royalty check.

APPLICATION 8-4 (46)

Have I written a textbook? Should I? How can I improve?

TEXTBOOK SUPPLEMENTS AND REVIEWS

Books and edited books can be supplements to textbooks. Let's face it, textbook supplements like Instructor Manuals, test banks, PowerPoint slides, and others and writing a review of a textbook are not highly rated for tenure and promotion and you will not get rich writing supplements or textbook reviews.

However, *publishing supplements* generally pays a decent set rate and you are guaranteed a non-refereed publication upon the agreement with the editor. Both writing and reviewing give you and your school some name recognition—reputation and they are both professional activity, which may be classified as service in your school evaluation system.

Completing *textbook reviews*, however, is generally not considered a publication even though you do a written book review (typically answer questions) because the review is used to make a decision to publish a new book and to get ideas to improve textbooks. But it does pay a decent set rate and you usually do get your name and school listed in the acknowledgements of the textbook.

Also, publishing supplements and writing textbook reviews gives satisfaction and pride of contributing to the successful teaching and outcomes assessment of thousands of students, possibly world-wide. In fact, I started writing skill exercises to accompany textbooks and it led me to textbook writing. I'm still writing the Instructor's Manual supplement for my textbooks, and I'm very grateful to many reviewers for their ideas that have improved my textbooks. As stated in the preface, if you have ideas on how to improve this book, I'd like to hear from you.

If you want to write textbook supplements or textbook review, just contact the author of a book you want to work on, such as one you use to teach with or the publisher stating your interest. If you do get an interested publisher, don't forget to let the editor make the first compensation offer. Don't be afraid to ask what other textbook supplement writers and reviewers doing the same work as you are getting paid. You can also work for multiple publishers and compare compensation.

APPLICATION 8-5 (47)

Have I written a textbook supplement or textbook review? Should I? How can I improve?

_____

_____

_____

_____

SUMMARY OF TIPS

- You can publish informative editor-selected articles for practitioners.
- If you ask, you may be able to change an editor-selected article to a refereed journal article.
- Practitioners don't really want a literature review, detailed methods, or advanced statistics; they do want practical implications that they can use on the job to improve performance.
- Contact editors and ask if they are interested in your topic for an informative article, or ask them what topics they are interested in publishing.
- You can publish an article for academics and another article for practitioners.

- Practitioners like case studies that state how an organization implemented a managerial process with recommendations on how they too can use the best practice.
- When writing for practitioners keep it short and concise, use easy to read and understand vocabulary, give lots of examples, and use lots of headings and bullets.
- You can get a publication by editing a book.
- Through conference contacts, you could edit the proceedings.
- If you edit a book for sale, be prepared to negotiate compensation from your publisher and to your contributing authors.
- If you are a contributing author to an editor of a book for sale, be prepared to negotiate your compensation with your editor.
- When negotiating compensation, let the other party make the first offer.
- You can edit, or be a contributing author, to an academic edited book, generally without compensation.
- You can write a book review for an editor selected publication, usually the book review editor makes the publication decision.
- If you have a book, try to get it reviewed for the publicity to increase sales.
- Contact book review editors and either ask them if they are interested in a review of a book you read, or ask for a list of books of interest to be reviewed.
- When you do a book review, include a complete reference, introduction to the book, give the contents of the book, present the highlights, and evaluate both its strengths and weaknesses.
- Writing a textbook is an entrepreneurial venture; risky with no pay check only royalties.
- Textbooks need a competitive advantage to get accepted for publications.
- To get a contract to write a textbook, generally, you will need to write a prospectus and 2–3 sample chapters.

- Larger and smaller publishers have different advantages and disadvantages, and going with larger publishers is generally more lucrative, but not always.
- You can write textbook supplements for compensation and editor selected publication.
- Writing textbook reviews is not a publication, but it is professional activity and pays compensation.

CHAPTER 9

EMPIRICAL RESEARCH

CHAPTER OVERVIEW

In this chapter, I discuss the major parts of an empirical research article in the common scientific format or structure. For more detailed information on this chapter, see my *Research Methods and Statistics for Business* textbook (Waveland Press).

Thus, this chapter serves as a reference guide outline or template to follow when conducting and writing your research. In addition to the template, it explains the important elements to include in each section of the article.

- In the first section, I discuss the importance of selecting a title and keywords to improve your chances of getting your article accepted, and then cited by others.
- The second section focuses on the abstract. The abstract gives the reader a first impression, which influences the acceptance or rejection decision. After publication, the abstract influences if the article will be read and cited by others.
- In the third section, I explain why the introduction section has to answer the so-what question, including the four parts you need to include to the answer the question.
- The forth section provides tips for writing the review of the literature and hypotheses.
- In the fifth section, I describe the four parts of the methods section.

- The results section focuses on discussing your finding, including hypotheses testing, using statistical terminology.
- The last section describes the five areas that should be included in your discussion section.

CHAPTER OUTLINE

TITLE AND KEYWORDS

It is important to select a good title using keywords. Doing so not only helps get your article accepted, it also helps get it cited.

Selecting the Title and Keywords

When you do empirical research, you should have two objectives in mind. First, you want to get the article published. Secondly, you want to have your article read and cited by others; this is especially true in schools with publication requirement that your work be cited. The title and keywords you select to use in your article help with the acceptance, but more so with getting your article read and cited because people will find your work based on its title and keywords. Therefore, the title and key word selection is an important decision that should be addressed from the beginning.

When you start your empirical research article with a proposal, it is a good idea to select a title and keywords to be included in the title, abstract, and throughout the article. You get ideas for the title and keywords when you do your literature review. What are the keywords you used to find the articles you cite in your article?

Although you start with a title and keywords, after completing the literature review and again after writing the article you should rethink and revise the title and make sure to select keywords carefully. What are the titles and keywords used in the articles you cite in your article?

Your title should accurately describe what your article is about. The title should also include your keywords. One question to ask yourself is, do my title and keywords match the literature?

Getting Cited

To get your article read and cited by others, address these realities. When people search, they commonly use keywords.

Therefore, you need to use the keywords that will result in your article being found. When people do a search, article titles are the first thing they see. They make the decision to read or download your article based on the title. So will your article title get the searcher's attention and be selected to include in their work?

Here is another point to keep in mind. Search engines rank the relevance of articles based on the use of keywords or phrases appearing in the title, keywords and abstract, and how many times the keywords are used throughout the article. So to come to the top of the search list, using the correct keywords is critical. Therefore, consistently use the words and phrases that are the most important, or although some people like variety, don't vary your use of keywords.

APPLICATION 9-1 (48)

Do I select my title and keywords carefully? How can I improve?

ABSTRACT

The abstract is a concise summary of the essential facts of the article. Getting back to our two objectives, the editor and reviewers will read your abstract and make a first impression; so make it a good one. Secondly, after people do a search and find your article by its title and keywords, the next common step is to read the abstract to determine if your article will be cited in their work.

Abstracts are also used as a proposal to write a paper for a conference or as the bases for selecting papers for conferences. Therefore, the abstract is critically important to publication acceptance and citation. Although it commonly appears as the first section of the article, it is written last.

Here is a general guide for writing the abstract. It is common to provide the information following the headings of the article in sequence. Start by stating the purpose or objective of your article from your introduction. Move to briefly stating the methods and sample, followed by your results. End with a discussion of your implications.

Most sources of publications will provide some guidelines for writing the abstract. Some journals, including *Emerald*, require headings. However, many sources only list a range or maximum number of words the abstract can include. Be sure to stay within the word count because if you don't your abstract might be cut in mid-sentence without your ending. Match your abstract with those of others in the target journal.

After writing the first draft of the abstract, do a word count. You may be over the limit and need to cut it back. Regardless of its length, because the abstract is so important, I spend time writing and re-writing the abstract and all coauthors do the same. We make sure the abstract includes our keywords, essential facts, and that it flows well to get the reader interested from the start. As with the entire article, do a good job of proofreading (Chapter 2).

APPLICATION 9-2 (49)

Do my abstracts include keywords, essential facts, and does it flow well to get the reader interested? How can I improve it?

INTRODUCTION

The introduction needs to answer the so-what question by including the importance, need for research, purpose, and implications.

The So-What Question

As with the abstract, the introduction has to get the editor and reviewers, and then researchers, interested in reading your article. To do so, the introduction has to answer the so-what question. The so-what question can be different depending on who wants the answer. The editor and reviewers are asking, what is so good about your article that I should accept it for publication? A potential reading of the article is thinking, I'm busy, so what is so good about your article that I should spend my time reading it?

If your introduction doesn't do a good job of answering the so-what question, the odds of your article being rejected increase dramatically. After acceptance, a good introduction leads to your article being read and then cited. Let's list and discuss the four parts that need to be including when answering the so-what question.

Importance, Need for Research, Purpose, and Implications

Because it is so important to include the four parts, let's review answering the so what question again using a different format.

- *Why* is your topic and study *important?* Why is there a *need for the research?*
- *What* is your *research question, purpose* or *objective?* What is the significance of your article? What is the gap in the literature that you are filling? What new knowledge are you adding to the literature? What is your original contribution?
- *Who* will be interested in the answer to your research question? Who can benefit from your *implications*: researchers, practitioners, consultants, educators?

I can't overstate the importance of the abstract and introduction. Here are some dos and don'ts when writing your introduction to answer the so what question.

- *First.* Unlike the abstract, the intro should be written first, but you should come back to it for revisions after completing the article.
- *Heading.* The introduction may or may not have a heading. Check the headings of the target journal to match it.
- *Inclusion.* All four parts (importance, research question, need for research, and implications) should be included in your introduction.
- *Sequence.* The sequence of the parts that answer the so-what question can be changed to fit your style and study. For example, you could start with a question such as, why do some businesses fail and others succeed?
- *Short.* Two or three concise paragraphs should be enough to answer the so-what question.
- *References.* Do include references to support your introduction.

APPLICATION 9-3 (50)

Do my introductions answer the so-what question? How can I improve?

_____

_____

_____

_____

LITERATURE REVIEW AND HYPOTHESES

Your literature review is a description of the literature that is the foundation for your research study. It gives an overview of prior research. It is common to present the literature with the hypotheses supporting your tentative answer to the research questions.

Your literature review should develop a theory. To make a contribution to the literature, your idea needs to be articulated, organized, connected in a way that suggests new directions for researchers, and fills a gap in the literature. Ideas are not a theory, regardless of how original they are. To be a theory, ideas have to be presented with a clear logic and causal relationship among the variables studied.

Here are some dos and don'ts when writing your literature review:

- *Keywords.* Do use keywords when searching for the literature you will include in your review.
- *Target journal.* Do review and emulate the literature reviews of articles you cite, and match the target journal literature reviews.
- *Hypotheses.* Do format your hypotheses in the same way as the target journal articles (Chapter 4, Matching Publication Sources).
- *Relevant.* Do cite all the "relevant" articles that relate to your study. An article is not a dissertation, so don't reference irrelevant articles.
- *Reference chain.* Do follow the reference chain (Chapter 3) to find all the relevant articles pertaining to your study.
- *Empirical.* Do your literature review citing primarily empirical research articles, or keep the use of books and newspaper and magazine articles to a minimum. Some conceptual articles are also acceptable because of their strong literature review, but get the empirical articles the authors cite.
- *Current.* Do have up-to-date references; not doing so make the topic look outdated and without need for your research.
- *Synthesis.* Don't just list prior studies one at a time in separate paragraphs. Compare and contrast the articles. How were the prior studies methods and results similar and different?

- *Add.* Do add comments and bring out themes and trends and make conclusions.
- *Gaps.* Do state the significant questions in the literature that your study addresses? Finding contradictions in prior research identifies gaps indicating the need for your research.

The last two points, Add and Gaps, are placed at the end of the literature review as a summary and conclusion. However, this information is also needed in the introduction of your article. The introduction is shorter with fewer references, but it essentially says the same thing in different words than the longer, more detailed conclusion to the lit review.

APPLICATION 9-4 (51)

Do my literature reviews do a good job of developing theory and describing how I fill a gap in the literature? How can I improve?

_____

_____

_____

METHODS

The methods section describes your research design, the participants and procedures of data collection, the variables and how you measured them, and the statistical analysis you ran to test your hypotheses. Although the content of two of these heading is short, I keep them separate because they are commonly-used headings in business research.

Research Design

Data Collection

The primary research design is based on how you collect your data. There are three categories of data collection for empirical research studies:

- *Secondary.* Is your data taken from recorded information? For example, are you using stock market prices, company records, or a database like the census?
- *Survey.* Is your data taken by developing a questionnaire and asking people to answer the questions in personal interviews, telephone, or mail/email interviewers?
- *Observation.* Is your data collected by watching the behavior of some phenomenon?

Other Dimensions

Here are some other design considerations to include in your statement of the research design:

- *Type of study.* Is your design conclusive or exploratory? If it is exploratory, you usually say so, but not for conclusive as it is assumed to be conclusive if not stated otherwise.
- *Time dimension.* Is your design cross-sectional or longitudinal? If it is longitudinal, you usually say so, but not for cross-sectional as it is assumed to be so.
- *Environment.* Is your data collected in a lab or in the field? If it is a lab, you usually say so, but not for field work.

Participants and Procedures

Who are the participants and what procedures did you follow to collect the data? When using survey research, the sampling procedures need to be stated clearly. The total sample size must be clearly stated and the response rate percentage given. For example, 200 surveys were mailed and 25 were returned as non-deliverable. Of the 175 surveys, 65 were returned. Thus, the sample size is 65 with a response rate of 37%. You can also provide percentages of descriptive statistics, such as men and women or by type of business.

It is common to include descriptive statistics to give the reader an idea of the participants. If target journal articles include descriptive statistics tables, include them. Although procedures are always discussed, the word procedures is not commonly used in the subheading of business research articles.

Measures

What are your dependent and independent variables and how did you operationally define them? Are the variables nominal (male or female), ordinal or interval (scales of say 1–7 disagree to agree) or ratio (age) levels of measures?

Statistical Analysis

Based on your variables and their measurement levels, what statistical test did you run to test your hypotheses? You can run multiple statistical tests for your study. Five common statistical analyses include:

- *Tests of Difference.* Comparing the value of one dependent variable across two or more levels of one independent variable; income of men and women (t-test).
- *Tests of Interaction.* Comparing value differences between one or more dependent and one or more independent variables (at least three variables) while also looking for the best combination of variables; income of men and women and type of job (two-way ANOVA).
- *Test of Association.* Correlating two or more variables; income and age (Pearson R).
- *Test of Prediction.* Predicting the value of one dependent variable based on the values of one or more independent variables; GPA by IQ and SAT scores (Multiple Regression).
- *Test of Interrelationship.* Reducing a large number of variables into a limited number of factors; reasons people select a college (Factor Analysis).

APPLICATION 9-5 (52)

Do I do a good job with the methods section? How can I improve?

_____

_____

_____

_____

RESULTS

The results section is relatively shorter than the literature review, methods, and discussion sections. You assume that the reader is knowledgeable about statistical analysis. The focus is on presenting the major statistical findings and the results of hypotheses testing using appropriate statistical terminology.

It is common to present your results in one or more *tables.* Check with your target journal to match the format and the content for your statistical analysis. Although you include tables, you must state the more important findings in the results section.

This section describes the results of your *hypotheses testing.* The one thing that is nice about inferential statistical analysis is that the important bottom line probability value (p-value), also called the *level of significance,* is always the same. The smaller the p-value, the greater are the odds that you are not making a Type I error; saying there is a relationship between your variables when there really is no relationship. The commonly used p-value is .05, so if your p-value is equal to or less than .05, there is at least a 95% probability that you are not making a Type I error.

Thus, when you test the alternative hypotheses stating there is a relationship between your variables, and the p-value is less than .05, your statistical analysis supports your hypotheses, and when it is greater than .05, it does not support your hypotheses. For example, Hypothesis 1: Men have higher levels of income than women. The p-value/level of significance from the computer printout is .0213. Therefore, Hypothesis 1 is supported. There is a 98% probability that there really is a difference in the income levels of men and women in the sample, or there is only a 2% chance of a random sampling error.

APPLICATION 9-6 (53)

Do I do a good job with the results section? How can I improve?

_____

_____

_____

DISCUSSION

The discussion, also called conclusion, section has five important topic areas to include, presented below. However, check and match your target journal for the use of headings and subheadings. Thus, you may or may not want to use the subheadings below or you may want to change the sequence of the discussion subheadings. You may want to combine some of the headings. I often combine the discussion of the study limitations with further research suggestions to help overcome the limitations.

Findings

In the results section, you presented the findings using statistical terminology. Now in the discussion section you assume that the reader has no knowledge of inferential statistics so you present the results in common everyday language. Assume you are presenting your results to a first year college student that never had a course in statistics.

You wrote a great introduction stating your research question, purpose, or objective of your study. Now you tell the reader to what extent you answered your research question. To what extent did you achieve the purpose or objective of your study?

Compare to Literature

You included a great review of the literature stating the results of prior research studies. Now it is time to compare prior study results to your current study results. Clearly state if your results supported or did not support each of the important prior studies. As in the lit review, synthesize by combining the prior studies that did and did not have the same results.

Getting back to the introduction to your study, you claimed that your topic was important and that there was a need for your research. Did you fill a gap in the literature? Now you tell the reader about your contribution to the literature in more detail?

Limitations

Your findings focus on the present state of your topic and the comparison of your results to the literature updates the topic for the reader. But the limitations subsection shifts the focus on the boundaries or restrictions of your work.

Although we all like to think we completed a great research study, the reality is that ALL research has some limitations. You need to state some of the more important limitations to your study. If you were a reviewer of the article, what limitations would you come up with? What limitations do you think the actual reviewers will think should be included? Your lit review should help you with this section. What limitations did prior studies have that your research also has?

Further Research

Remember that when you write empirical research articles the primary audience is academics. Researchers want to know what recommendations you have to continue this research topic. Recall (Chapter 3) that the further research section of articles is a place to look for research topics, and it also provides support for the importance and need for your research. So making suggestions for further research is an important part of your article. You can help other researchers and have an impact on the future direction of your topic. Think in terms of now that you completed the study, what would you do differently in the future to improve the research?

Recommendations for further research are important when the results of prior studies are mixed. If there were five prior studies and two and three had different results, and you support the two prior studies, at this point there is no clear agreement. If you have the first article with the topic, or are the first with results that are contrary to prior studies, other researchers need to conduct studies to provide more evidence to conclusively support your findings. Thus, when there are contradictions in the literature and new topics, there is a need for further research.

What aspect of the topic do you think still needs more work? What other related research questions need to be answered? Your lit review should help you with this subsection. What recommendations for further research did prior authors have that your research did not fully address but still need work?

Implications

There has been a call to make research more relevant to practice. Therefore, many editors and reviewers require a good discussion of the implications of your study. In the introduction to your article, you answered the so what question by briefly stating who can benefit from your study and how. The implication section is not just a repeat of the introduction.

In this subsection, you get into the details of your implications for research on the topic. Describe how researchers, practitioners, government, educators, consultants, and anyone else can benefit from your research. With practitioners, break them down into separate groups. For example, you can state how a business itself and its customers, suppliers, investors, and bankers may benefit. With the government, what recommendations do you have for public policy makers? How can consultants do a better job of helping their clients, and how can educators do a better job of teaching their students? Once again, your literature review should help you with this subsection. What implications did prior authors present that are also relevant to your study?

APPLICATION 9-7 (54)

Do I include the five subsections of the discussion section? How can I improve?

_____

_____

_____

_____

SUMMARY OF TIPS

- Review target journal articles for ideas on what to include in each section of the empirical research article, and to match the format of target journal (Chapter 4).
- Select an article title that describes your research including your keywords.
- Choose keywords carefully based on the literature so that your article will come to the top of a search, increasing your chances of getting your article cited.
- Make sure your abstract is a concise summary of the essential facts of the article, and that it flows well to get the reader interested from the start.
- Your introduction must answer the so-what question.
- The parts of the so-what questions include: why the topic is important, the need for your research (gap in the lit), the purpose of your study, and the implications stating who can benefit from your study.
- Start by writing your introduction, keep it to 2–3 paragraphs while including references, but the sequence of the four parts to answering the so what question can vary.

- Follow the reference chain (Chapter 3) to find all the relevant articles pertaining to your study.
- Write a great literature review by citing the current relevant empirical articles related to your study.
- Do a synthesis of prior studies, add comment and bring out themes and trends and make conclusions about the literature, and state how your research fills gaps in the literature.
- Your methods should clearly state your research design stating your data collection.
- If your research design is exploratory, longitudinal, or conducted in a lab, say so in your research design description.
- Be sure your methods include a description of your participants and the procedures you used to collect the data, including the total sample size and response rate.
- The dependent and independent variables, with their operational definition, must be stated with their level of measurement.
- The specific variables to test each hypothesis must be clearly stated with the statistical test used to determine if the hypothesis is supported or not.
- The results section should focus on presenting the major statistical findings and the results of hypotheses testing using appropriate statistical terminology, including *p*-values with tables.
- The discussion section should clearly state your findings in non-statistical terminology. Discuss to what extent did you answered your research question and achieve the purpose or objective of your study?
- You discussion should compare the results of your study to that of prior studies. Describe your contribution to the literature; what gap did you fill?
- All studies have limitations, and academics want to know what further research is recommended on your topic, so include a discussion of both.

- Editors and reviewers want to know who can benefit from your research, so include a discussion of your implications for everyone (researchers, practitioners, government, educators, consultants), who can use your findings.

LaVergne, TN USA
30 July 2010
191535LV00002B/23/P